Praise for *Messy Minimalism*

"*Messy Minimalism* gives us permission to do minimalism our way—
the way that best supports our families. This book shows us the
imperfect way, the messy way, and, most importantly, the real way.
Rachelle Crawford's gentle approach makes minimalism and living a
more joyful life approachable for everyone."

—Courtney Carver, author of *Project 333* and
Soulful Simplicity, and founder of Be More with Less

"Rachelle Crawford will make you breathe a sigh of relief at your
normalcy (you know, the mess we all have), and she'll hold your hand
toward a doable life of less, honoring your humanness along the way.
Best of all, she'll feel like an old friend, the one you can call for advice.
I've got her 'on speed dial'—on my bookshelf."

—Melissa Coleman, author of *The Minimalist Kitchen*
and founder of The Faux Martha

"With grace, authenticity, and humor, Rachelle Crawford shows readers
that living clutter-free isn't solely reserved for the perfectly organized.
This is a witty and wise must-read for anyone looking to exchange a life
distracted by stuff for more joy, presence, and calm."

—Joshua Becker, author of *The Minimalist Home* and
other books, and founder of Becoming Minimalist

"By providing an honest, practical approach to decluttering, Rachelle
Crawford redefines minimalism as a lifestyle that is attainable and
achievable for anyone wishing to pursue it."

—Christine Platt, author of *The Afrominimalist's Guide to Living with Less*

MESSY MINIMALISM

MESSY MINIMALISM

Realistic Strategies for the Rest of Us

Rachelle Crawford

Broadleaf Books
Minneapolis

MESSY MINIMALISM
Realistic Strategies for the Rest of Us

Cover image: Adobe Stock
Cover design: Cindy Laun

Print ISBN: 978-1-5064-6686-6
eBook ISBN: 978-1-5064-6687-3

Portions of chapter 17 appeared in a guest blog post "Getting Decluttered with Your
Significant Other," *Becoming Minimalist* (blog), September 21, 2020, https://www
.becomingminimalist.com/getting-decluttered-with-your-significant-other/.

Printed in Canada

For my children, Jameson, Raegan, and Amelia.

You remind me every day that our best
moments are typically the messiest ones.

CONTENTS

CONTENTS

PART III DECLUTTERING YOUR SPACE

PART IV LIVING WITH PURPOSE

FOREWORD

Messiness had been a part of my life for as long as I can remember. For my first thirty years, I was drowning in stuff. I have a fast-moving brain that leads me from one thing to the next, and so I left a trail of evidence behind me along the way.

Seven years ago, then, as a newly married young mother, I felt like I was accumulating *people* just as fast as I was collecting stuff. My chaotic schedule frustrated the people I loved the most, but I was unsure how I could make a change to show my growing family a different way.

If you are a messy person reading this, you know the struggle to put things away and throw things out or give them away. Or if you are messy with regard to schedule and commitments, you know how hard it is to tidy your calendar and learn to say no. Indeed, if you're like me, you've never dreamed that minimalism was something that would work for you.

Yet minimalism has changed my messy life.

On this journey toward a simpler life, I met Rachelle Crawford, author of the book you hold in your hands. I quickly learned that Rachelle and I are kindred spirits. I'm thankful to Rachelle for writing this book. She and I are living proof that messy people can be minimalists too. In fact, I would argue that minimalism is *especially* for us messy folk—because no organizational system will do the trick. We don't need a better way to organize and store all the stuff; we just need *less* of the stuff.

But before you dive in, I want to give you a warning. Rachelle's wisdom won't end when you finish cleaning out your closet. Instead, you are going to find that minimalism has a trickle-down effect. You may be starting in your kitchen, but before you know it you'll be simplifying your calendar, decluttering your mental load, and living your whole life with more intention. I suspect you will come to find a sense of lightness that you never thought possible. Minimalism is infectious in the best sort of way.

Cheers to an imperfect yet simpler life! This book is a gift that will bring you guidance, inspiration, and self-acceptance.

—Denaye Barahona, PhD, Simple Families
and author of *Simple Happy Parenting*

PART I

BECOMING MINIMAL-ISH

AN OUTLANDISH IDEA

Maybe the life you've always wanted is buried under everything you own.

—Joshua Becker

I don't like the word *minimalism*. As a self-declared minimalist, I'm probably not supposed to say that, but there you have it. While I love everything minimalism truly stands for, the word itself? Eh, not so much.

Minimalism has that all-or-nothing ring to it, as if embracing it requires an unwavering, cultlike devotion. As if you must choose between a colorful wardrobe or a bland one, between having a family or living solo out of a VW van. The first thing a friend said to me when I told him I was going minimalist was, "What? Are you going to get rid of your couches now?" As if minimalists must take a monk-like vow to never sit for the remainder of their uncomfortable, miserable lives.

I get it. From a distance, minimalism can appear extreme, uninviting, and even coldhearted. If you google "How to become a minimalist," you'll quickly come to learn it's a *whole thing*: a movement of people from all walks of life who want out of the overconsumption game. There are zero-waste minimalists, cozy minimalists, essentialists, extreme minimalists, and those who are simply living minimal-ish. You can read about entire families living out of RVs, singles living out of backpacks, and retirees downsizing to only the bare essentials.

For the longest time I figured minimalism was either for cool people willing to live in uncomfortably bland, big-city lofts or those committed to deprivation, discomfort, and boredom. It just seemed unattractive, unattainable, and absolutely unsustainable. This is exactly why for so long, I assumed it wasn't for me. I mean, I do like to sit from time to time, preferably on a comfortable couch.

Besides, life is just too short to settle for "less," right? It's meant for living abundantly—to the fullest and even overflowing. That's exactly what I did. I filled our home until we were bursting at the seams.

Now, just in case you're reading this and thinking, "Lady, you keep using this word *minimalism*, but I'm not sure what you mean," let me explain. Minimalism is the purposeful practice of paring back both our material possessions and commitments in order to create a greater capacity to invest our time and energy in the things that matter most.

I had no idea it was possible for *real* people to implement minimalism in their everyday lives. My preconceived ideas about what minimalism meant kept me from even considering the very thing that, in fact, I desperately needed.

I had spent my entire life living an exact opposite lifestyle, holding on to everything, paring back on nothing. I would need to first meet a real live human, intentionally and joyfully living with less, before I could wrap my brain around doing this myself.

Thankfully, that's exactly what happened.

FINDING LESS

That morning started off like most mornings. The only difference was this was the second Wednesday of the month, which meant I was at my church moms' group, soaking up some kid-free time, coffee, and cream cheese with a side of bagel.

This week's speaker was here to share tips for healthy meal planning while, ironically, I stuffed my face with a week's worth of calories. Thankfully it was a judgment-free zone because I was ravenous. As per usual, I had spent that morning scrambling to get my older two kids out the door for school and the littlest ready for church. There would have been barely enough time to shower, pop my hair into a messy bun loaded with dry shampoo, and down a cup of coffee. I most certainly hadn't had time to eat breakfast.

> *I had no idea it was possible for* real *people to implement minimalism in their everyday lives.*

Life back then was one big juggling act. I lived in the land of busy at all times, constantly working to get caught up while tripping over the endless piles of stuff in my very, very cluttered home. I figured clutter and chaos just came with this motherhood gig.

The speaker began to share with us how she feeds her family of seven. (Yes, that's a grand total of five children!) I really don't remember much of her talk because of an aside she made partway through. She went from talking about batch-chopping veggies to moving her family across the country after one of her parents became ill.

She concluded her heartfelt sidestep with the statement: "Thankfully, the packing wasn't too difficult because we're minimalists."

At that, I dropped both my pen and my jaw and let out an audible gasp. Sitting straight up in my chair, I waited to hear another gasp echo mine. I glanced to the people at my table and then began scanning the room. Had anybody else just heard what I had? My heart started racing, and in that moment I immediately began to feel lighter.

"So wait," I thought, "you can be a mom and a minimalist? You don't have to keep everything, for everybody, for all of eternity? She has five flipping kids! I have only three and I'm drowning here."

For the remainder of the meeting, the speaker's voice sounded, in my head at least, a bit like Charlie Brown's teacher: "Wah wah *waaaahh* wah *wahh*." Frankly, I didn't hear another word. I just sat there, picturing my home without all the clutter. With every passing second I grew more and more hopeful that maybe, just maybe, I wasn't so bad at adulting after all. Maybe I just had too much crap!

Once the meeting closed, I power walked my way to the back of the room as that speaker poured herself a cup of coffee. "Stay calm, Rachelle," I thought. "Don't be a weirdo." My internal pep talk had little effect, and I immediately began to bombard her with question after question. How? What? When? For a second I debated kidnapping her and bringing her home to help me minimize my possessions, but I figured my newly uncluttered home would do me no good if I ended up in prison. Instead, I settled for the online resources she shared with me.

After grabbing my then one-year-old from childcare (God bless those childcare workers), I picked up my middle child from preschool and headed toward home. It was almost lunchtime, so I figured I'd give my husband a little ring to prepare him for this 180-degree turn our family was about to make. As I explained where we were headed, he listened quietly before following up with his usual response, "Yeah, let's talk about this tonight," which, in my experience, is code for, "Did you seriously just call me at work to discuss such nonsense?" In his defense, I have been known to get overly excited about outlandish ideas. I'm still waiting for him to agree to the idea of our moving overseas for a few years (but let's be clear: I'd settle for a couple weeks).

Something about this particular outlandish idea was different, though. I could feel it. For the first time, I was hopeful there was a reason that, for so long, I'd felt an irrational dissatisfaction with my seemingly perfect life. Perhaps the solution was much simpler than I thought.

Perhaps the answer wasn't found in doing more, spending more, or being more. Maybe the answer was hiding behind *less* all along. Could all of my efforts to keep up, outdo, reorganize, and redecorate actually be the root of my problem?

GROWING OVERWHELMED

The year or so leading up to our transition into minimalism was full of change—mostly good change, but change nevertheless. I've always been one who prefers things to remain exactly the way they are forever, amen. But after eleven years as a labor and delivery nurse, I had decided to stay home full time with our three kiddos. Yes, I wanted to spend more time with my little ones and cherish those younger years—isn't that what "good moms" are supposed to say?—but deep down, I was hoping that I'd finally, *finally*, get a grip on our homelife.

When my oldest, Jameson, was born, I had gone from full time to part time. When my middle child, Raegan, was born, I went from part time to per diem, working even fewer hours. While I was cutting back more and more at work, our house remained a disaster. Getting dinner on the table practically killed me, and we were on the go constantly.

> *Perhaps the answer wasn't found in doing more, spending more, or being more. Maybe the answer was hiding behind* less *all along.*

With the birth of my youngest, Amelia, I finally resigned altogether. I turned in my epidural cartridge key, emptied my locker, and trashed my reliable yet wildly contaminated pair of Dansko clogs. Heading off the floor for the last time, I figured I had just uncovered the secret to a perfectly managed homelife.

Yeeeaaahh, if you've ever been a stay-at-home parent for even just five minutes, then you're probably silently mocking me right now. Go ahead, I deserve it. Yes, stay-at-home parents *are* physically home more; however, they are also *physically home more*. The mess was only made worse by my being at home all the time, and my inability to tidy didn't improve at all. Now there was simply no escaping it.

When I was working in labor and delivery, I got to be the hero. I was the one with a direct line to the anesthesiologist at all hours of the night. But at home, I was just that crazy lady who kept begging people to put their shoes and toys where they go. I mean, how hard *is* it?

I thought opting to stay home meant that I was going to have all of the time in the world to exercise, tidy up, organize our space, and teach my little ones how to be polite, at least in public. When I realized that scenario was as likely as a *Seinfeld* reunion, I felt like a failure.

> *I had been living a cluttered life and didn't even know it because managing and maintaining stuff is just what we do.*

Over the course of that first year home full time, I worked hard to keep my head above water, maintain a grateful heart and a present mind. After all, not everybody has the opportunity to stay home full time with their babies. I so badly wanted to get it right.

Yet with each passing day I grew more overwhelmed at the state of my home and more underwhelmed by the trajectory I saw my life headed. Was living in survival mode really all there was to this season of life?

I vividly recall an evening just a few months prior to my headfirst dive into minimalism. The sense of overwhelm began to overtake me. It all felt meaningless. My husband and I were sitting in our living room, likely watching a movie or scrolling through our phones at the end of an exhausting day of the same ole, same ole. I remember looking around at our living room—the same one I had cleaned a dozen times that day, as evidenced by my signature piles at the edges of the room (more about those in chapter 2). And I was just *over* it. I was over the constant cycle of picking up, sorting toys, and hurrying from one commitment to another. But on top of that, I was over living a life so focused on the accumulation and maintenance of stuff. I desperately needed to get off the hamster wheel, but I didn't know how.

I recall feeling as though the walls were closing in around me. I could hardly breathe. I wanted to run. While deeply in love with my little family, I wanted to flee the scene of this life we'd been living. I couldn't put my finger on the problem, but deep inside I knew there was one.

I wondered if this perhaps was what they call a midlife crisis—though I wasn't at all wild about the idea of thirty-four marking my midlife. When I couldn't shake away the overwhelm, I considered the possibility that the subtle hum of worry I'd experienced my whole life was now turning into a full-blown case of diagnosable anxiety. Was I just losing it?

It is said when the student is ready, the teacher will appear, and only a few weeks later I found myself sitting in that auditorium. The case for less had slowly been building within my heart, preparing me for the message of minimalism I so badly needed.

It took me thirty-four long years to learn that I had a too-much-stuff problem, not a me problem. I had been living a cluttered life and didn't even know it because managing and maintaining stuff is just what we do. We accumulate everything from novelty napkins and silverware caddies to shoes for every possible occasion, all in an effort to simplify our lives and live more comfortably. Ironically, overconsumption often has the exact opposite effect. What we hope will simplify our lives and create a more comfortable and aesthetically pleasing home can, in fact, be the very thing causing us to feel so overwhelmed.

January 18, 2017, was the day it all changed for me. That was the day I set off on a journey to not only right our family's course but to share the benefits of owning less with anyone who cared to hear about them. Within the month I started a blog called *Abundant Life with Less*, a fitting title for the journey I was on. What began as an overcomplicated way of holding myself accountable has grown into a passion, with thousands of readers from all over the world and all walks of life. While on one hand it was rather amazing to watch its reach grow, I can't say that I was all that surprised. Not because of me—I had no idea what I was doing. For the longest time, my website was pretty much held together by the internet equivalent of hot glue. I wasn't surprised because I knew I wasn't the only person in need of this message. I wasn't the only one who was also absolutely over it. The transformative power of the clutter-free life can be pretty contagious.

Friend, if you're over it, you're in the right place. *Messy Minimalism* is here to escort you off the hamster wheel. If you aren't so sure if minimalism as you know it is for you—well, you're probably right. Minimalism, *as you know it*, probably isn't for you. I'll go ahead and spoil the end of the story now: turns out it wasn't for me either. My messy, real life just couldn't keep up with the sparse, immaculate, perfectly curated images typical of minimalism. I would need to redefine it for myself, which is how messy minimalism was born.

> *The transformative power of the*
> *clutter-free life can be pretty contagious.*

I wrote this book to share with you a doable, practical, relatable approach to living a clutter-free life. Ironically, the many misconceptions cluttering up the concept of minimalism are keeping people stuck in their clutter: overwhelmed, overly busy, and broke. Here you'll find a simpler approach, one that allows you to embrace both the mess *and* a life of less.

So if you're ready to ditch either the excess *or* the idyllic version of minimalism you've been pursuing—or perhaps both—I wrote this book for you. Let's get started.

2

REDEFINING MINIMALISM

Your home is meant to hold what matters to you and your family. If something doesn't matter, it's taking space from something that does.

—Kendra Adachi

Do you remember those optical-illusion posters from the 1990s? I know: I try to block all things '90s from my mind as well. We survived the extra-wide-leg jeans fiasco only to dive headfirst into bell-bottoms. It was almost as if we didn't want dry pant legs. It couldn't have been all bad, though. Scrunchies, crop tops, and tie-dye are back and better than ever—at least for now. They'll probably be long gone by the time this book gets to your hands. On top of my evolving sense of style, eventually

I stopped singeing my bangs into a perfect cylinder, figured out that my Lebanese eyebrows need to be tweezed, and learned my hair is actually curly, not just a pile of frizz. All it needed was a little product. Who knew?

> *Once I saw my excess stuff for what it was,*
> *I couldn't get rid of it fast enough.*

Anyway, as I was saying: optical-illusion posters were all the rage. If I remember correctly, there was even an entire store at our local mall dedicated to the sale of such posters. At first glance, they just looked like fuzzy pictures of colorful nothingness. If you didn't know any better, you'd walk right by without giving them another thought. Yet if you gave it a minute—maybe squinted a little, relaxed your eyes, moved toward and then slowly away from the picture—in time, the real image would appear. One moment you'd be staring at a blur, and the next a pod of dolphins would be diving out of the poster at you.

Another strange thing about those posters was that once you saw the hidden image—once you knew what it was—you couldn't *un*see it. What took forever to come into focus the first time took just seconds every time after. Once you saw it, it became so obvious you'd wonder why it took you so long to see it in the first place.

For many, finding minimalism is a similar experience. You can't unsee it. Once I saw my excess stuff for what it was, I couldn't get rid of it fast enough. I dove in headfirst, decluttering my home with a vengeance and wondering why it had taken me so long to get here. Why had I held on to so much stuff for so long? Why had I spent so much time accumulating colorful piles of nothingness?

CLUTTERED BY NATURE

Have you ever witnessed someone do something completely new or different and then thought to yourself, "Yes! That totally sounds like something so-and-so would do"?

Yeah, nobody thought that about me and minimalism. In fact, my declaration was met with laughs and eye rolls.

I don't blame my family and friends for doubting me. Minimalism isn't exactly a natural fit for me. If you've read *The Life-Changing Magic of Tidying Up* or watched the reality show *Tidying Up with Marie Kondo*, then you know all about the incredibly organized minimalist guru behind the KonMari Method who has been tidying spaces since she was a child. Me? I'm the opposite. For every room Marie has organized and tidied, I've cluttered and untidied an equal number. When I was a child, my family joked that you could follow my trail of stuff around the house to learn exactly how I had spent my day. I imagine my parents were speaking the truth because I have since raised three children who have inherited this skill.

> *I had been confusing an abundant life with a cluttered one, ultimately allowing my overconsumption to suck from me the very life I was trying to build.*

I've always lived a cluttered life. My parents kept everything. Their parents kept everything. My sisters and I (you guessed it) kept everything. Clutter was just a normal part of homelife. Growing up, I had a purse, doll, and book collection. I held on to every movie stub, every project, and every note passed to me during science class—which was a lot (just ask my science teacher, Mrs Kessler). Everything was sentimental. Everything was important.

When my parents would ask me to clean my room, I'd simply form multiple piles of stuff along the walls of my bedroom. If I could clear a reasonable amount of space in the center of my room, I felt my efforts were a success. My college dorm life was mildly better, and that's only because a human who was unrelated to me needed to share my space.

So at the time I found myself sitting in that mom group, I was the most cluttered person I knew, holding the title of Least Likely to Ever Become a Minimalist. It made no sense, and the odds of me pulling it off were not in my favor.

Thankfully that speaker showed me a better way, suggesting I look again, this time with a little more intentionality. What I saw was that my mantra of "more, more, more" was causing me to settle for a life distracted by stuff, in pursuit of all the wrong things. I had been confusing an abundant life with a cluttered one, ultimately allowing my overconsumption to suck from me the very life I was trying to build.

My home isn't the only thing that has changed since that day. Less stuff is just the tip of the iceberg once you pursue a life of minimalism. In my experience, it does not take long before everything else comes into focus as well.

THE TROUBLE WITH MINIMALISM

I know, I know. The title of this section might seem like a pretty abrupt about-face. Just a few sentences ago, I was singing the praises of minimalism, and now I'm about to reveal its dark side? We can't *not* talk about it, though. My hope is that by addressing it early on, I can help you avoid the same fateful missteps I took and equip you to spot the red flags of this common minimalist pitfall.

I had stumbled into minimalism the good old-fashioned way: word of mouth. But the more I researched, read, scrolled, and watched, the more I learned just how idyllic a minimalist home could become. As I looked for the best methods for becoming a minimalist, I found the internet loaded with an endless supply of images portraying the cleanest, clearest, most clutter-free homes imaginable. Perfectly organized kitchen pantry essentials neatly arranged in mason jars. Tidy kids bedrooms peppered with toys in muted tones without a Disney character in sight. Large, trendy mudrooms boasting hooks and cubbies for every household member.

With minimalism gaining in popularity and growing as a movement, there was simple-living inspiration everywhere I turned. It looked so peaceful, so calm, so perfect—which led me to assume that peace and calm were just on the other side of perfect. It all felt out of reach. Although that didn't stop me from trying to get there.

We spent our weekends and evenings culling through our excess, delivering load after load to our local thrift store. We carted away the toys my kids never played with, a vegetable spiralizer we hadn't even used once, piles of clothing that hadn't seen the light of day in years, and boxes filled with the most random vases and gaudy tableware. Never before had I felt so light. Month after month we worked, moving through our home on a mission to ditch the excess. For the first time in my life I was creating systems and routines that left my home functioning in a rhythm of order.

I was now able to wash, fold, *and* put away our laundry on the same day. All of our kids' toys actually fit in their respective bins and boxes. For the first time in my adult life, I had a meal plan for our family. Me! A meal planner! We could now tidy our house in a matter of minutes and woke up every morning to a clean kitchen. Slowly my home started to reflect the minimalism I pictured in my mind. Now that we had less stuff, all of our possessions had a place, and everybody in my home knew where it all went. I was in heaven.

And then our dishwasher broke.

REMOVING MINIMALISM FROM ITS PEDESTAL

On one regular Sunday afternoon, my husband pushed a little too hard when closing the dishwasher door, snapping a critical part in half. With what I admit now to be *great* hyperbole, everything started to fall apart. I felt like I was watching an apocalyptic movie in which one wrong move causes a beaker to spill over, thus unleashing a chain reaction of nuclear-meltdown proportions. I stood there in our kitchen, looking at my husband's face, as the gravity of what he had done sank in.

In that one moment, a wrench was tossed into the gears of my efficient routines and systems. Slowly and simultaneously they all began to crumble to the ground. Life spiraled out of control, almost in slow motion, and suddenly I was looking at a mountain of laundry, an overflowing pile of dishes, and three wild children pulling everything off the shelves and tossing things strategically at my feet while I wandered helplessly in circles. I couldn't keep up. It was complete and utter anarchy.

A broken dishwasher is hardly reason for a total meltdown, but I know you've been there too. When something small undoes you—your husband accidently takes your keys to work with him or your five-year-old spills an entire cup of milk that somehow manages to flow into the unreachable cracks between the cabinet and the refrigerator—those minor infractions can result in a disproportionate response, especially when you're already hanging on by a thread.

In the days that followed what should have been just a simple mishap, I started to reconsider minimalism entirely. Was it really an attainable or sustainable lifestyle for me and my family? Maybe it was best to leave this minimalism thing to the single hipsters or the countercultural rebels living in vans down by the river. Perhaps I needed to just walk away and let the cluttering commence. How could one broken dishwasher part bring my minimalism crashing down around me?

The problem, however, didn't lie with minimalism itself. Nor were my dishwasher, systems, routines, or rhythms to blame. Those can all be really great things (especially the dishwasher—I'm a big fan). The guilty party here was me, and the pedestal on which I had placed minimalism.

> *I had become entranced with perfection, forgetting that the minimalist way of life is ultimately about* purpose.

What this broken dishwasher revealed was that my minimalism had become as much about holding on as it was about letting go. Except it wasn't material possessions I was holding on to anymore; it was control. Deep down, I was hoping that the perfect implementation of minimalism would safeguard me from hard times and permanently protect me from those feelings of suffocating overwhelm I had struggled with for so long.

Having found minimalism as the solution, I now thought it imperative to my well-being that I implement it exactly right. Somewhere along the way I had gotten turned around. I had become entranced with perfection, forgetting that the minimalist way of life is ultimately about *purpose*. My number-one goal had become making my minimalism look the part.

What had begun as me doing "a little helpful research" in hopes of learning more about this new lifestyle quickly escalated into a race to the finish line. I had become hyperfocused on curating an Insta-worthy living space while ignoring the deeper internal work that needed to take place first. I hadn't paused to consider whether or not those picture-perfect images even fit my real life.

HIDING THE SNARL

The other day my eight-year-old had a video call with her class while remote learning. A few minutes before I needed to sign her into the online meeting, I noticed her hair was a disaster. I started brushing but quickly realized this was going to take some work. It was a snarled mess! With just a minute left, I said to her, "You know what? I'm going to just brush the front and then we'll deal with the back later. Nobody will see it."

And that, right there, is exactly what I did during those first few months of minimalism. Yes, I dug deep, reaching to the back corners of closets and through the dust balls beneath our furniture to pull out the physical clutter. But in my effort to get it looking perfect fast, I brushed right over the larger issues tangled under the surface of my heart. The very reasons that led me to the cluttered life in the first place.

Perfectionism is a sneaky little thing and, when left unchecked, becomes a way of life. Couple perfectionism's ability to lurk in the shadows of everyday living with the quantifiability of minimalism and, well, you've got a recipe for disaster. Minimalism had become a numbers game for me, and I want to make sure it doesn't for you. Every item we removed from our home felt like it moved us one step closer to perfection, peace, and calm. Instead of making minimalism my own and letting it serve the real life I am called to live, I had white-knuckled some ideal version I found on Instagram and pursued that, slowly idolizing it in the process.

> *Nothing built on a foundation of comparison, perfectionism, and unrealistic expectations can stand for very long.*

Picture-perfect minimalism is an exhausting journey that will get you nowhere fast. In fact, as it turns out, the pursuit of minimalism can be even more distracting than the cluttered life I was used to. Perfectionism is the very reason so many of us get stuck and turn back before ever making any real progress simplifying our lives. Sure, perhaps we can pull it off long enough to start a blog, share a few photos on social media, and leave our friends and family in awe of our bare closets. But nothing built on a foundation of comparison, perfectionism, and unrealistic expectations can stand for very long. These things are sandy soil, my friend. As I learned the hard way, it doesn't take much to bring the perfectionist life crumbling to the ground.

I'm so glad mine crumbled, though, because it gave me a second chance to do things differently. To rebuild on a foundation of grace and authenticity.

STARTING FROM SCRATCH

After that broken dishwasher broke the camel's back, we took a good couple of months off from our decluttering efforts in order to get really clear on what it was we were truly after. Was this really worth it? If so, how could we implement minimalism in a way that best served *our* family in the everyday messy moments as well as the tidy ones? How could we make minimalism serve our real lives instead of us serving it?

What should have been an insignificant hiccup had wrecked my best intentions and revealed a need to overhaul the way we were implementing this major change in course. If minimalism was going to have the positive impact we hoped for, we'd need to redefine it for ourselves.

What slowly began to emerge was a grace-based form of minimalism I call *messy minimalism*. Messy minimalism is the practice of minimalizing our minimalism. It's letting go of getting it perfect in exchange for a clutter-free life unique to you and your often messy life.

Here's a helpful formula if you need to see it mathematically:

$$(\text{Minimalism} - \text{Perfection} + \text{Sustainability}) \times \text{Grace} = \text{Messy Minimalism}$$

Messy minimalism is a flexible form of minimalism that acknowledges our humanness and any natural tendency toward messiness and honors our inability to control all the details. It makes room for dishwashers that break and children who drop more food on the floor during dinner than lands in their mouths. It makes room for aging parents who need us, seasons that require more from us, and school projects covering our dining room table for weeks on end. Messy minimalism frees us to love our sticky counters, acrylic paint–stained dining tables, and the spaghetti-sauce handprint adhered to the window. It honors our goal of permanently decluttering our space while accommodating our real lives that, at times, get in the way of that progress.

> *A messy form of minimalism allows me to be me, my family to be them, and life to occur as it will.*

On top of all that, it makes room for the people in our homes who may not be as into the idea of living clutter-free as we are. A messy form of minimalism allows me to be me, my family to be them, and life to occur as it will. It's the practice of letting go; I mean *really* letting go.

If you're at the end of your rope, done trying to maintain a perfect image of minimalism that doesn't really suit you anyway, there's a better way. A way of grace. A version of minimalism that isn't at all concerned with the way it looks from the outside but rather with the way it transforms your home—and your heart—from the inside. At the heart of it, minimalism isn't really about the "stuff" at all. It's simply an outward expression of a deeper, more inward transformation. Messy minimalism involves a process of pulling back the layers, brushing out the snarls, finding who it is you were created to be, and then becoming exactly that.

3

THE MESSY MINIMALIST WAY

To be yourself in a world that is constantly trying to make you something else is the greatest accomplishment.

—Ralph Waldo Emerson

Just in case you haven't picked up on this yet, I can be a bit of a slob. My initial instinct has always been to walk away from a mess. I'm all about letting pans "soak overnight." Messy minimalism has done little to change that.

It has, however, allowed me to create an environment I am much more capable of managing. Just as you should never give a toddler an open jar of glitter, neither should you give a messy person twenty-four pairs of jeans, sixty-eight T-shirts, eighteen bras, and thirty-four pairs of shoes. It's a recipe for disaster.

Sure: some people embrace minimalism because they are naturally inclined toward tidiness. But it's us messy people who need minimalism most of all.

I am the kind of girl who leaves cabinet doors open as I move about the kitchen. I rarely put the cap back on the toothpaste, and when I change into my pajamas at the end of the day, most of the time I just drop my clothes on the floor—and by most of the time, I mean all of the time. Eventually I'll get around to hanging them up or tossing them into the hamper, but it certainly won't be upon undressing. Tidying up always takes a back seat to Netflix.

On top of my own messiness, I have a family. My husband is much tidier than I, but our three children seem to have inherited my not-so-tidy genetic makeup. Deep down, I used to bank on motherhood automatically turning me into the tidy person I've always longed to be. I assumed I'd arrive home from the hospital with a baby in my arms as a new woman, transformed into Mary Poppins overnight. That was not the case. I never have managed to pull a hat rack out of my diaper bag—just the usual smashed-up Gerber granola bar adhered to a long-lost onesie. In fact, a propensity for messiness often gets worse after you become a parent. You have less free time on your hands while more and more is required of you.

So we've never had a particularly tidy home—though I do feel it's important, for the sake of my pride, to differentiate between "messy" and just plain "dirty." While yes, our flooring is 50 percent KIX, wooden blocks, and craft supplies, I do regularly deep clean my home. There's no need for a tetanus booster if you plan to stop by—just slippers because there are LEGO bricks and pipe cleaners everywhere.

THE MESSY MINIMALIST WAY

The fact of the matter is this: neither motherhood nor an idealistic version of minimalism was ever going to magically turn me into something I wasn't. While minimalism chants simplicity, the version I had been chasing did anything but simplify. When I found my new conversion to minimalism faltering under the weight of my unrealistic expectations for perfection, I had three choices. I could try harder. I could abandon the cause. *Or* I could swap those unrealistic expectations for a kind of minimalism that worked for me. Thankfully, I chose door number three.

> *Messy minimalism is still minimalism, just minus all the unrealistic expectations, preconceived ideas, and endless pursuit of unattainable perfection.*

Over time, like breaking in a snug pair of jeans, my minimalism began to stretch and shape, developing wider seams and adjusting to fit the very real and often messy life I lead. I'm still the same messy person I've always been; I'm just more self-aware these days. According to my husband, I still can't properly load a dishwasher to save my life. And I'll always moonwalk away from the scene of a mess, intending to "clean it up later." My home still gets messy. But everything now has a place, once we get around to putting it away.

Listen up: you don't need to be a messy person to embrace the messy minimalist way. This is about sustainability. Messy minimalism is still minimalism, just minus all the unrealistic expectations, preconceived ideas, and endless pursuit of unattainable perfection. It's for real people, living real lives, which occasionally get messy. It's for the person who wants clear kitchen countertops and a bit of breathing in their home—but also knows it's only a matter of minutes before their five-year-old finds a hole puncher and transforms one simple sheet of construction paper into a dining room covered in confetti.

A minimalist lifestyle isn't reserved for singles, hipsters, or empty nesters. You won't be forced to grow a man bun or trade your stilettos for Birkenstocks. (Though, in my opinion, Birkenstocks are *absolutely* the way to go.) You don't need to sell your home in the suburbs and move into a three-hundred-square-foot tiny home in the woods. You can paint your walls whatever color you'd like, *and* you can even keep your kids! Heck, those kiddos can even keep their Disney Princess dolls. There is no need to swap out all of their beloved toys for the eco-friendly, Montessori ones. There isn't an exact number of clothing items you should own or a list of things you're not allowed to buy. Nor do you need to sacrifice your favorite hobbies in exchange for "slow living."

Like I said before, becoming a messy minimalist isn't about becoming someone else altogether. It's about unearthing who you really are beneath the mounds of clutter, overconsumption, and the chaotic pace we've been told equates to a meaningful life.

THE MESSY MINIMALIST MANIFESTO

In essence, this is what messy minimalism stands for:

- Less is more; so much more.
- Minimalism is a guardrail, not a destination.
- I am not concerned with how my minimalism appears on the outside but how it transforms me from the inside.
- This is not about deprivation but rather prioritization.
- I know decluttering is a process that takes time, and that's okay.
- My pace is my pace. All progress counts.
- Owning less stuff reduces decisions and distractions so that I can create for myself a greater capacity to be present each moment and live purposefully.
- I'm not in this to conform my space to fit some idealistic, cookie-cutter version of minimalism.
- Messy minimalism is about laying down what I don't need so that I am free to pick up what I do.
- Life is about more than a series of purchases.
- I am an uncluttered person meant to live a clutter-free life.
- I maintain a teachable posture, knowing I don't have it all figured out.
- Minimalism is here to serve me and my real, often messy life. Not the other way around.

At the core, minimalism is simply a tool to help you live a purposeful life with fewer distractions. What matters in the end isn't arriving at the finish line with the fewest items in your arms. Life isn't a numbers game. We are simply choosing to carry along fewer things so that in the end we find ourselves holding only the things that truly matter.

As we move through this book together, it's important to note that my messy minimalism will look different than yours. Yours may be a bit tidier or perhaps even a little bit messier. This is a judgment-free zone, friend. Please don't consider this book to be a formulaic, step-by-step process; you're not defusing a bomb. It's more like a choose-your-own-adventure book. The journey you take through the land of less may wind in a completely different direction than mine has. All I hope is that in the end, you find yourself confidently on a path toward a more meaningful life, doing exactly what it is you were created to do. The world depends on it.

Now a word on effort.

EVERYTHING IS "FIGUREOUTABLE"

As I write this, it's been approximately one year since I strummed my very first chord on the ukulele. The C chord, to be precise. At the ripe old age of thirty-seven, I decided to learn to play the ukulele.

This wasn't my first attempt to learn an instrument. When I was a child, my parents signed me up for piano lessons. It was a total bust. They insisted I'd regret stopping lessons when I grew up, but I didn't care then, nor do I care today. I'm sure there are plenty of people out there who regret not continuing their piano lessons as a child. I am not one of those people.

My sweet parents then doubled down a few years later and signed me up for guitar lessons. This, too, was a failure. My disinterest may have been, in part, due to the fact that my "well-seasoned" guitar teacher's playlist included songs like "Cripple Creek" and "Go Tell Aunt Rhody." They were both painfully repetitive songs, and Aunt Rhody? Well, she got to hear it from me that her ole gray goose was dead. Grammy-worthy lyrics for sure.

I can't solely blame the instructor or the song list. I'm just not a musical person. I have a terrible singing voice. This ukulele story isn't like one of those teen rom-coms either—you know, where the "nerdy" girl with glasses finally gets contacts, tweezes her eyebrows, and straightens her hair to reveal that she's actually the most beautiful girl in the school. No. I can sing about two or three notes fairly well. Anything above or below that octave and I sound like Scuttle from *The Little Mermaid*. The only people ever lucky enough to hear me sing are my family, road-trip comrades, anyone within a ten-foot radius during my *Hamilton* phase, and the lucky churchgoers in the pew in front of me when the worship team spontaneously halts the music and I, well, just keep on singing. Awkward.

So when my daughter came to my husband and me and asked if she could learn to play the ukulele, I first checked her for a fever. Then I figured it was something we should probably take seriously.

I don't know if it was a more relevant playlist, how easy her teacher made it look, or the challenge of it all, but during my daughter's first lesson, I became determined to learn alongside her. I mean, how hard could it be?

After learning a handful of chords from the back of the room during her very first lesson, I went home and did what any newbie with a ukulele does: I googled the chords to "Somewhere over the Rainbow" and hit Play on YouTube. It took me all of two seconds to realize just how in over my head I was. Not only were the chords changing faster than my fingers could move, but I was shocked to discover just how difficult it is to simultaneously sing with your mouth, strum with one hand, and change chords with the other. The sound that filled our home was *painful*. Just ask Paul.

But I kept on driving my daughter to her lessons, sitting in the back, and paying more attention to her instructor than she did. Every few days I'd pick up that ukulele and practice what we—I mean she—was learning. I started air-strumming along to songs as I ran errands, practicing coordination and rhythm, most of the time without even realizing I was doing it. My fingertips started to grow callouses as playing the ukulele became a part of my self-care routine—as well as a great tool for procrastinating.

I had no end game: no plan in place, no real reason to learn the ukulele besides simply wanting to. But guess which song I just learned to play and sing at the same time? In the privacy of my own home, of course. Yeah, that's right. "Somewhere over the Rainbow."

As kids, we're often taught that it's now or never. "You'll regret it when you're older," the adults say. As if once you're older, that's it: there's no more growing. No more learning. Sure, I grew up an unmusical, disorganized hoarder of movie theater ticket stubs; but that's not who I have to be forever. You have it in you to make the shift, change your thinking, do hard things, and awaken new dreams.

Learning the ukulele at the ripe old age of thirty-seven has taught me three things.

First, one year will go by, regardless of what you do with that time. Where would you like to be a year from now? Whether it's playing the ukulele on your couch or getting ready for work in front of your now-minimalist closet, what you do today will determine where you are then. The changes you make can be subtle, simple, even minuscule, as long as they are purposeful and consistent. I didn't spend hours a day playing the ukulele. (You're welcome, Paul.) I wasn't looking to become the next sensation. I just loved the ukulele-playing version of me, and I wanted to be more like her.

> *You have it in you to make the shift, change your thinking, do hard things, and awaken new dreams.*

Second, while I'm not naturally musically gifted, I discovered that, in the words of author and entrepreneur Marie Forleo, "Everything is figureoutable." If you're staring at what feels like too much stuff for one person to ever declutter, know this: you have what it takes. I know you do. It may not happen as fast as you'd like, and it will certainly suck more than a few weekends from your calendar. But you're not meant to live your life drowning in clutter. You, friend, are an uncluttered person, and you'll figure out a way that works for you.

Third, it's only figureoutable as long as, in the words of author Jon Acuff, you're "brave enough to be bad at something new." As you begin to let go of the clutter that's weighing you down and holding you back, the process will ebb and flow between exhilarating and exhausting. Remember: you're just getting your sea legs. I had practiced overconsumption and accumulation for thirty-four long years before becoming minimalist. Turning that tide doesn't happen overnight. (Well, I guess a tide does technically turn overnight, but you get the point.) Your pace is your pace. Every step, however small, is still forward progress.

Trust me, dear reader: if I can unclutter my life, you can too. As evidenced by my bedroom when I was ten, my college dorm room when I was twenty, and my home when I was thirty, I'm the last person you'd ever expect to not only become a minimalist but write a book about it.

If minimalism is feeling a little outside your wheelhouse, you're in the right place. Stick with me, and I'll show you just how figureoutable it can be.

4

START WITH WHO, NOT *WHY*

Some things we have to become before we can do them. . . .
Activity always follows identity.

—Jeff Goins

Since the earliest days of my minimalist journey, I've been helping others embark on their own. Instant expert? Hardly. I was more like an overly enthusiastic declutterer of crap. If you live near me and I'm confident you're not a murderer, I'll likely say yes if you ask me to help you minimize. The promise of coffee is the only real requirement here. It's a good day in the life of Rachelle when she gets to help someone else make big strides toward minimalism. I've helped people declutter everything from clothing and kitchens to DVD collections and basement storage areas. I've pretty much seen it all.

Since early 2017, I'd been writing on the subject of minimalism, speaking at events, and creating digital resources, all to help people get started and stay motivated as they unclutter their lives. There was just one problem. I was missing the most important first step.

You see, I believed minimalism was born out of a big aha moment, like the one I had at that Wednesday morning mom group. I assumed making the shift from an overabundance of stuff to a minimalist lifestyle required either a hard fall to rock bottom or a profound lightbulb moment. As if the right amount of inspiration could offer enough momentum to propel you through a lifetime of purposefully living with less. That's exactly what I *thought* had happened to me.

So as I began to help other people make steps toward minimalism, I taught them that their very next step, after deciding to go minimalist, should be to write out *why*. I referred to it as a "Why Statement." Clever, I know. If their minimalism was going to stick through the highs and the lows, I told them, they would need to get something down on paper to reflect on. When the going got rough and their motivation waned, they'd be able to refer back to their Why Statement for inspiration.

Someone's Why Statement might include wanting to spend less time cleaning and more time soaking up memories. Someone else's Why Statement might include their hope to pay off their home, eliminate debt, and give more generously to those in need. Whatever your reasoning for making this shift into minimalism, it needed to be big, and it needed to be personal.

A Why Statement makes sense, doesn't it? It even sounds pretty.

Too bad it doesn't work.

WHY "WHY" DOESN'T STICK

The problem is this: wanting something bad enough doesn't make it come to fruition. Knowing *why* you want to do something doesn't necessarily make you do it. What I've witnessed time and time again is that while aha moments, and the subsequent Why Statements, certainly provide the initial motivation and heartwarming epiphanies, all too often they stall out when the rubber meets the road.

People would declutter their space, and they'd be thrilled. They'd love the look, the feel, and even the sound of a minimalist home. After all, noise does travel differently in an uncluttered space. A few weeks later, though—when seasonal trends had changed or they happened upon a new line of decor at Target—they'd abandon all minimalist efforts in exchange for more stuff. While they were drawn to minimalism, it just wouldn't stick. They would declutter just enough to feel satisfied with their space and call it good . . . until a few months later, when the cycle of heedless consumption would start again.

What's the difference between those who keep at it, decluttering their lives with a vengeance, refusing to ever go back, and those who lose interest and once again start filling their spaces with things?

I didn't get it, and I began to search for the answer. I informally surveyed minimalists and wannabe minimalists alike, trying to figure out what it was that made minimalism stick for some and not for others. I sent out a questionnaire to a few thousand readers looking for the answer, hoping to uncover the common denominator causing some people, myself included, to stick with minimalism.

Because trust me: I'm not tougher or tidier. We've established that. Why was I able to make this major change in course? What's the difference between those who keep at it, decluttering their lives with a vengeance, refusing to ever go back, and those who lose interest and once again start filling their spaces with things?

All of my research came to a head the summer I started reading up on habits. It was then that I realized that true change doesn't start with the question of *why* at all. No, it starts with *who*. Shifting our habits over the long term first begins with a shift in identity.

GOAL-BASED VS. IDENTITY-BASED HABITS

I'm so grateful you're here reading this book right now. I know it's going to help you simplify your home and life and equip you to move through your days with greater purpose, grace, and joy. Once you finish reading this book, however, please pick up *Atomic Habits: An Easy & Proven Way to Build Good Habits & Break Bad Ones* by James Clear. Trust me, it's too good to miss.

To grossly under-summarize it, *Atomic Habits* is about developing and implementing small habits to ensure a more productive trajectory for your life. By developing even the tiniest positive habits, you can purposely set yourself on the right course to make big progress and reach lofty goals. Genius.

Yet while good habits are essential, that's not the part I want to point out to you. The part that stuck out to me as it relates to becoming a minimalist—or becoming anything, for that matter—was Clear's differentiation between two kinds of habits we can form: goal-based habits and identity-based habits.

Goal-based habits, Clear explains, focus on the end result you hope to achieve. For example, your goal-based habits might include losing twenty pounds, getting out of debt, or doubling your sales for the year. The steps you take and the habits you create will move you toward or away from accomplishing your goal. Say that your goal is to spend more time with your family, create a tidier living space, or save money by eliminating the cost of your off-site storage unit. You may be choosing minimalism as a means to get there. If that's the case, then decluttering and owning less would be the new—but potentially temporary—goal-based habits you might develop.

Identity-based habits, Clear says, are much stronger. These habits are developed as we shift our sense of who we are.

The ultimate form of intrinsic motivation is when a habit becomes part of your identity. It's one thing to say I'm the type of person who *wants* this. It's something very different to say I'm the type of person who *is* this.

> The more pride you have in a particular aspect of your identity, the more motivated you will be to maintain the habits associated with it. . . . Once your pride gets involved, you'll fight tooth and nail to maintain your habits.

When I read those words, I realized exactly how this drastic lifestyle change unfolded for me and why it stuck. You see, I've always wanted a tidier home. The Why Statement for my own life would have *always* included spending as much time with my family as possible and living a life that glorified God with everything I do, say, and have. My *why* was the same before and after minimalism. Writing it down wasn't going to make letting go of the things cluttering up my life any easier.

Instead, it was *who* I was created to be that suddenly became clearer. The life I had been living didn't line up with who I was. Yes, that delightful speaker, bless her, introduced me to minimalism on that Wednesday morning, and my *why* breathed hope into the task at hand. Yet it was a shift in identity that sealed the deal that day.

> *When your new minimalist lifestyle is founded on identity instead of a goal, you'll start to uncover skills and strengths you long forgot about.*

Those who stop their minimalist journey once their living room contains fewer toys have simply reached their goal. The clearer space has allowed them to obtain what it was they were after at that point in time. The drive to push forward just isn't there anymore.

It's a bit like a two-week juice cleanse. Your goal may be to detox, shed a few pounds, or jump-start your metabolism. Those are admirable goals—and a juice cleanse is certainly one way to live your life (says the girl eating a bag of Cheez-Its while she types). Creating a goal like this one isn't wrong. In fact, it can be very effective. However, it's highly likely that you'll need to set this same goal over and over again. It's not a long-term solution. The same thing occurs when we reorganize a cluttered space or join a decluttering challenge. Once we've met our goal, we no longer feel the need to maintain the behavior changes that helped get us there. All too often, it's just a matter of time until we find ourselves back at square one.

When your new minimalist lifestyle is founded on identity instead of a goal, you'll start to uncover skills and strengths you long forgot about. For example, you'll realize just how resourceful you are and find you don't really need to hop on Amazon and "add to cart" any and every new item on a whim. When you approach your space as a clutter-free person rather than a person looking to declutter, it changes the game altogether. You're now looking for ways you can put your home to work for you rather than continuing to live in service to your stuff. You're not simply decluttering your desk drawers; you're putting that desk to work for you for good. Your space should support the life you are meant to live. Let's not get uncluttered just for today; let's live uncluttered from here on out.

> *We can live uncluttered, undistracted lives—lives that are solely focused on the things that last—not because we're trying to become someone we're not, but because we're finally becoming who we were truly created to be.*

One of the questions I asked readers in that questionnaire was this: "Have you always had a natural tendency toward owning less? If yes, you absolutely fascinate me. How?! What is your biggest motivator?" Those who responded with yes typically didn't really know how to articulate it. They'd say something along the lines of "I've just always been this way." While at first those vague responses didn't really seem all that helpful, the more I thought about it, the more I started to see a theme. Those who have always preferred their spaces be simplified and minimized see it as a part of who they are. *This is just how I like things. This is just who I am.*

"Minimalism is a frame of mind," writes Erica Layne in *The Minimalist Way.* "It's a decision to, over the course of months and years, work toward a life that fits. A life that matches who you are inside—and somehow makes you even more." And Greg McKeown, author of *Essentialism*, has this to say on the subject of identity and the clutter-free life: "There are two ways of thinking about Essentialism. The first is to think of it as something you *do* occasionally. The second is to think of it as something you *are*. In the former, Essentialism is one more thing to add to your already overstuffed life. In the latter, it is a different way—a simpler way—of doing everything. It becomes a lifestyle. It becomes an all-encompassing approach to living and leading. It becomes the essence of who we are."

I want to be really clear here: when I suggest you make messy minimalism a part of your identity, I'm not suggesting you adhere your total value as a human to its execution. Being a minimalist doesn't define us. It's simply a slice of the pie. Minimalism is not who we are in our entirety. It's simply an effective method for letting who we truly are, and whose we are, take center stage in our lives. We can live uncluttered, undistracted lives—lives that are solely focused on the things that last—not because we're trying to become someone we're not, but because we're finally becoming who we were truly created to be.

TO THE "ASPIRING" MINIMALIST

By the time I got home that Wednesday afternoon, fed my kids lunch, and plugged them in to PBS KIDS, I had already, in my mind, *become* a minimalist. This wasn't just going to be my new method for cleaning or organizing my home. It wasn't even about eliminating the excess toys I loathed (though that has certainly been a perk). I hadn't yet decluttered a *single thing*. But this was the new me, and it went much deeper than my material possessions.

I wanted to be the kind of person who didn't need so much stuff in the first place. I wanted to be the kind of person who chooses to accumulate more memories in life than material possessions. The kind of person who gives more away than she holds on to. Who exhales gratitude and contentment rather than always looking out for something newer, something better, something different, something bigger.

If you're simply here in hopes of making enough room to park your car in your garage this winter, this book will certainly help get you there. But I fear you'll find your way back to clutter if you don't first make living with less a part of who you are.

> *Waiting to* become *a minimalist until you've fully decluttered your home is like waiting to call yourself a runner until the moment you cross the finish line of your first marathon.*

I was confident this new approach to material possessions was exactly what our home needed—and what my soul needed. If it was true for me, I'm willing to guess it's true for you as well. Less stuff, more space. Less hurry, more presence. That's what we're after here.

Waiting to *become* a minimalist until you've fully decluttered your home is like waiting to call yourself a runner until the moment you cross the finish line of your first marathon. It's like waiting to call yourself a writer until you've published a best-selling series that becomes a theme park. That's ridiculous. If you run, you're a runner. If you write, you're a writer.

The same goes for minimalism. Stop calling yourself an "aspiring minimalist" and start calling yourself a minimalist the moment you determine to live clutter-free. Your home may not look "minimalist" from the outside, but that's okay. In my experience, your friends and family will widen their eyes, maybe even nod and smile patronizingly when you tell them you've become a minimalist. After all, they've been inside your home. They've seen the way you stockpile various sizes of blenders on the counter as if your kitchen is an appliance store showroom.

So yes, there is work yet to be done. But you, my friend, are an uncluttered person, determined from here on out to live a life that reflects exactly that.

5

FINDING ABUNDANT LIFE

*It's a wild and wonderful thing to bump into someone and
realize it's you.*

—Fil Anderson

My husband, Paul, is a master at finding lost items. I think it just might be
his spiritual gift. Without fail he will find that lost stuffed puppy, missing
pair of pajama pants, and even the half sheet of blue paper containing
the date and time of our children's parent-teacher conferences. He
once found my wedding ring *inside* our DVD player. That one took some
next-level detective work, but he eventually figured out where our then
two-year-old had stashed it.

In our more than seventeen years of marriage, the only thing I recall
him not being able to find was his very own wedding ring. At first, we

weren't too concerned. After all, he had lost and found it before. He takes it off before bed every night and at work while typing, so really, it could have been in a number of places. However, when two months had gone by and he had scoured every nook and cranny of our home and his office, we had to accept the fact that his wedding ring was gone forever. If he can't find it, nobody can.

I, on the other hand, am the literal worst finder. If something of yours goes missing, don't ask me to help you look for it. I'm not the girl for that job. It could be sitting directly in front of my face and I just won't see it. I'll gladly join the hunt, but the odds of me being the one to find the missing item are slim to none. How about you just have me pick up coffee for the real search party?

This is why it was really no surprise that it took me thirty-four years to finally find my way to the land of less. While at first I thought the journey was simply about having fewer items to clean up every day, I quickly discovered that was only the beginning. The more you let go of, and the further you journey into minimalism, the more you'll find. Much of it completely unexpected.

Don't just take my word for it. While that questionnaire I sent to readers didn't lead me to discover a tangible common denominator in the lives of those who choose and stick with minimalism, what it did reveal was pretty fascinating—at least to people like me who nerd out on anything related to minimalism.

What this not-so-scientific study of mine revealed were three of the most common reasons people ditch their excess stuff and opt to intentionally live with less: to decrease stress and anxiety, to create more time, and to find financial freedom. Let's take a deeper look at each of these as well as a few other benefits to living as a messy minimalist.

LESS STRESS AND ANXIETY

Less stress and anxiety turned out to be the number-one reason the people I surveyed chose to go minimalist. Every response I read left me smiling and nodding in agreement because this was my biggest motivator as well. A decrease in stress and anxiety was the first thing I discovered after decluttering just one area of my home—well, that and my closet floor. One reader responded simply: "Visual clutter makes me feel uncomfortable and restless." Another shared these beautiful words:

> I was at a point in my life where I was feeling completely overwhelmed. I was having "health problems" which turned out to be anxiety that I refused to accept for a long while. On a much needed vacation, as I was in a much smaller space with many, many fewer "things," I realized how nice it was that I didn't have much to tend to or look after. Of course, there was less to do because it was vacation, but I specifically remember washing dishes in the tiny kitchen overlooking the family room where my husband and boys sat playing and thinking, "Wow! This is so nice. This is what life should be like." And so began the slow process of discovering minimalism and ultimately myself.

In 2009, researchers from the University of California, Los Angeles published the results of a study that identified higher levels of cortisol, the stress hormone, in women who perceived that their homes had a higher density of items. In other words, the more clutter women own, the more stressed out we are. It's science! All this time I had assumed my ever-rising sense of overwhelm had to do with *me* not being *enough*. I'd never paused to ask if, instead, my *stuff* was too *much*.

> *A decrease in stress and anxiety was the first thing*
> *I discovered after decluttering just one area of*
> *my home—well, that and my closet floor.*

When I couldn't find a missing shoe, or an important document went missing in a pile of meaningless ones, I'd place the blame on my own lack of capability. I'd wish myself to be tidier or more organized. If only I could figure out how to focus more, exercise more, pray more, and trust God more. If only I could go to bed earlier, then get up earlier, or systematize my day in a way that kept me one step ahead. I never paused to consider that perhaps stashing piles of stuff along the perimeter of my kitchen was actually adding to my stress level.

It wasn't until I started letting go that I was able to recognize just how much my clutter contributed to the stress and low-grade anxiety I felt on a daily basis. Turns out people who own fewer possessions report fewer home stressors. Who knew storing appliances, bread, and vitamins inside of your cabinets rather than out on the counters could have such a positive effect on your well-being?

Don't get me wrong. As you know, I've experienced firsthand just how problematic minimalism can be for your soul when you rely on it alone—when you take a good thing and make it the ultimate thing. Minimalism itself is not the pathway to peace. It simply creates a clearer path, leaving you with fewer items to trip over on your way there.

MORE TIME

Physicist Albert-László Barabási once said, "Time is our most valuable nonrenewable resource." But more time is exactly what people are finding as they enter the land of less: more time for the things that matter.

One reader shared with me that her family used to be so busy that "there was no time for us to be flexible." Another said, "For me the driving factor was to buy myself more time to do the things I loved." And another reader had this to say: "I find minimalism, in all areas of our lives, enables us to live simply and focus on what is actually important, to love others and to be loved."

I couldn't agree more. While time is nonrenewable, minimalism somehow seems to manufacture a few more hours in our week. Once we become less concerned with maintaining our culture's exhausting pace, it becomes easier to set our own and prioritize our lives in a way that leaves us more time in a day for the important things.

Here are just a few ways in which minimalism can give you more time:

- fewer errands
- elimination of busywork
- fewer commitments to extracurricular activities
- less time spent cleaning, reorganizing, and doing laundry

We'll talk about exactly *how* this works later in the book. For now, know that minimalism seems to slow down the hourglass and allow you more time to invest in the important things. What you do with your extra time will be yours for the choosing.

MORE MONEY

The third-place trophy in my mini-study goes to money. People are choosing to live simpler lives in an effort to reduce living expenses, pay off debt, and ultimately, save or give more money. The cost savings of a life less focused on the accumulation of stuff is significant. We started saving more money immediately—money we could redirect toward retirement, investments, college savings for our kids, generosity, adventures, and higher-quality, longer-lasting items.

> *We say the important things in life aren't things at all. Yet the way in which we spend our money—and ultimately our time in order to make that money—suggests otherwise.*

"My motivation for simplifying was debt," one reader shared with me. "I realized I wanted a different job but didn't feel like I could afford a decrease in salary because of my debt. In paying off debt, there was the decision to purchase less, thus shopping less and bringing in fewer items. The simplifying continued in other areas too."

Deep down we all know more stuff never satisfies. We say the important things in life aren't things at all. Yet the way in which we spend our money—and ultimately our time in order to make that money—suggests otherwise. Minimalism is freedom from that rat race. The minimalist crowd is full of people who have decided to take back the reins of their finances and no longer live beholden to debt.

Minimalism eliminates the need to keep up, ultimately allowing us to choose how we spend our money based on our long-term goals, not our immediate desires. It's delayed gratification put into action.

FINDING WHAT IS LOST

Speaking of money: if I had a quarter for every minute of my life I spent looking for lost items, I'd never have to work again. Not sure that math adds up, but you get the point. I've wasted so much time digging for my favorite jeans in a sea of uncomfortable ones, crawling around the closet floor to excavate my son's soccer cleat beneath the mound of random shoes, and scouring my daughter's dresser for the correct shade of pink legging to match her shirt. Serenity now!

Sure, we still lose things now and then. Our remote control is the most commonly misplaced item. (Why do they keep making them smaller and smaller?) But when you own less, you've got less to lose. As we cleared our home of clutter, I couldn't even begin to count the number of "favorite things" we found. Forgotten projects, beloved T-shirts, missing library books, and even a clay jar filled with actual money.

Over a decade ago, a family friend gave us a clay jar with the word *Blessing* inscribed on the side. The purpose of this Blessing Jar was for our family to slowly fill it with loose change. Once it was full, we would then use it to bless someone in need. I'm not sure exactly when we finished filling that jar with loose change, but eventually it made its way to the back of my husband's armoire, hidden behind stacks of shirts and piles of clutter. For years, that Blessing Jar sat there filled to the brim, accruing no interest, and blessing absolutely nobody.

We might as well have taken it out back and buried it. Instead of loving others with the resources entrusted us, we stored it right alongside our "What if I need it someday?" items. I used to think being a good steward of what I was given meant holding on to everything—you know, just in case. But that's not what we're meant to do at all.

What do you have tucked away, waiting to *maybe* get used someday, that someone else could use today? Don't be surprised if peace, time, money, and lost shoes aren't the only things you find along the way. It's all too easy to lose our sense of joy, generosity, contentment, and purpose in the fog of overconsumption.

AN ABUNDANT LIFE

I'm going to give it to you straight. While minimalism will simplify your life, it isn't always so simple. What began as a quest for less unlocked a world of wonder. One moment I was in my wardrobe, pushing my way through old cardigans and shirts that dated back to my college years. The next moment I was standing in Narnia, with everything I've ever believed to be true in question.

Keenly aware that I could never go back to my old way of thinking, I began asking myself if there were any other misconceptions and preconceived ideas I had let hold me back. If I'd had *this* wrong all this time, what other assumptions of mine might not add up?

> *If I'd had* this *wrong all this time, what other assumptions of mine might not add up?*

As I continued along on my journey toward less, I was surprised to discover a world of complexity along the way. This not-so-simple life kept challenging my assumptions about myself and pressed me to transform areas of my life that, for so long, I let operate on autopilot. It sparked a personal growth journey in me, one that will certainly never be complete. From the way I view my Christian faith to the new pie crust recipe I started using: everything in me has shifted, even just a little bit.

You see, this minimalism is a tricky thing. She waltzes in dressed as simplicity, and the next thing you know she has unraveled your soul. There's nothing simple about it. While at first glance minimalism seems to be all about your stuff, I've found it really has very little to do with your stuff. Turns out this is about so much more than reducing stress and creating more time to play UNO! with your kids. Sure minimalism will lead to that—lots of that!—but it will also reveal a deeper issue of the heart.

> *What if a rich and satisfying life doesn't require*
> *accumulating more but giving it away?*

I still remember exactly where I was when I made the connection between my faith and minimalism. I wasn't at church or reading my Bible. I was simply jumping around in my living room to an online workout video. Which one? I don't recall. But I began to wonder how far this could reach. I'd tasted and seen what cleared-off countertops could do for my home, and I was ready for that same peace to infiltrate every part of me. In John 10:10 Jesus said, "I have come that they may have life, and that they may have it more abundantly." For as long as I can remember, I was under the impression that an abundant life had to do with more: more comfort, more success, more money, nicer stuff, a better life, better health. Suddenly I found myself second-guessing all of it.

What if an abundant life has nothing to do with the accumulation of more but everything to do with letting go? What if the abundant life is found when we let go of our need for self-preservation and keeping up with the Joneses? What if we could loosen our tight hold on fear and worry and exchange it for deeper trust in God's provision, presence, and peace? What if we could swap our abundance of stuff for an undistracted life of purpose? What if a rich and satisfying life doesn't require accumulating more but giving it away?

Eventually, as our family embarked on this minimalist journey, we not only found that Blessing Jar full of coins; we eventually got around to putting it to good use. Together as a family we decided to pour out our offering into a coin-exchange kiosk that weekend and use the money to buy hats, mittens, boots, and coats to stock our school's winter-gear drive.

The evening before, I had reached to the back of that newly uncluttered armoire and grabbed a hold of the clay jar. It was surprisingly heavy. As I pulled it close to me so that I could carry it with both arms, I glanced down. There, sitting right at the top of the jar, camouflaged beside coins of a similar size, was my husband's long-lost wedding ring.

I was speechless. I'm not a crier, never have been, but I got close that day. I guess I was partly in shock because I'm never the one to find anything, especially something we were certain was gone forever. But mostly I was shocked at the profound moment before me. We had found our own treasure, hiding in the very thing we were meant to give away.

Minimalism offers us a chance to pick up what we've lost.

How long might that ring have remained hidden had we not chosen to finally let go? Had we not decided to use the blessings entrusted to us to fill the needs of others?

The messy minimalist way is one of generosity. Here we look around for both the things we have in abundance and the needs we can directly meet with them. In return, minimalism offers us a chance to pick up what we've lost.

I can't say for certain what that will look like for you. Perhaps it's discovering clearer counters, your son's favorite joke book, or a symbol of love in a jar of coins. Just don't be surprised if also hiding beneath the clutter you uncover lost dreams, creativity, contentment, generosity, a long-lost sense of adventure, and life to the full.

PART II

THE MESSY MINIMALIST MINDSET

COMBAT THE WHAT-IFS

God placed the best things in life on the other side of fear.
—Will Smith

I love a good infomercial. Not because they're effective but because they're comical. Seriously, how hard is it to flip a pancake with an ordinary spatula?

I want you to know that I'm not here to infomercial you into a life of less. Minimalism isn't a one-size-fits-all wearable blanket or a new indoor grill promising to forever improve every aspect of your life immediately upon purchase. While everything feels different around here, everything is also pretty much the same. My kids still argue. Their rooms are a mess, regularly. We get strep throat, things break, life happens, and apparently even global pandemics occur.

I didn't become a minimalist and then have every single day after become easy-peasy, tidy, and perfectly organized. Not hardly. My days are just a little easier-peasier, tidier, and somewhat more organized. Minimalism has lightened my workload, that's for sure, but more importantly, it's changed the way I think.

A few chapters from now, we are going to get down and dirty as we discuss practical strategies for getting that clutter out of your home. But first we need to unpack the way we think about material possessions. In this section of the book we are going to begin to develop a messy minimalist mindset. If we were to bypass our thought processes and spending habits in order to fast-forward to the decluttering process, our efforts to live an uncluttered life would become nothing more than another seasonal declutter—a Band-Aid, not a long-term solution. They wouldn't hold up during rough terrain, and they certainly wouldn't do us one bit of good when life throws a curveball.

CURVEBALL

May 1, 2020

I like to consider myself a well-prepared person (read: worst-case scenario expert). But even I didn't see this coming. Not at all. I don't think anybody did. What started off as a pesky virus on the other side of the world grew to become a worldwide pandemic.

Here I am on Blursday, at around day number 4,815,162,342, and this quarantine life just won't quit. I've received quite a few messages from friends and family asking me how my minimalism is holding up right about now. As if the closure of libraries and the inaccessibility of items such as hand sanitizer, poultry, and flour have managed to undo my minimalism. It's a good question, one I wrestled with myself during those first couple weeks of quarantine. I wondered if we'd gone too far. Would we regret having minimized our possessions? Would we need back a few of those extra sweaters I'd donated to barter with during the end of the world?

I can't be certain what the next few years will hold or what the world will be like when this book gets released. Believe me, I've certainly tried to speculate. But I'm more confident than ever that, pandemic or no pandemic, this messy minimalist life is exactly what we need.

If nothing else, this time of uncertainty has shone a light on the things that are truly essential. Suddenly we're all a little less concerned with which style of sandal is "in" this spring or which wall colors are trending right now. Instead, we are simply trying to keep our families safe, ensure we all have the food we need, and somehow convince our parents to stay the heck home. For the love!

This is our "someday." To the what-ifers, the just-in-casers, and the you-never-knowers like myself: this is it. This is that "What if I need it someday?" moment you've been holding out for as a way to avoid giving up your stuff. If you come through this global pandemic and economic crisis not having needed those what-if items, I'd be willing to bet you're never going to need them.

> *Let us* never *forget the time when we craved*
> *human connection over new shoes.*

At first glance it might seem as though *more* stuff would have left us better prepared for these unprecedented times. But it's just not the case. It's not more stuff we need right now. Instead it's hope, contentment, gratitude, peace, community—even if only from a distance—and trust in a faithful God who isn't at all surprised by our sudden change in circumstances.

In a matter of months we went from a record-setting economy to teetering on the brink of the Great Depression 2.0. While I'd certainly love for things to get back to normal sooner than later, I can't help but wonder if the whole idea of "back to normal" should even be on the table. We've got a second chance to get it right this time. Let's not miss it.

Let us *never* forget the time when we craved human connection over new shoes. When our basic needs became the focus of our attention and everything else was moved to the back burner. We know better now. We've had a firsthand encounter with the fragility of life as we know it. Let's never get all the way back to normal. Let's stop just shy of our entitlement, overconsumption, and our insatiable addiction to busy.

WHAT IF?

I didn't develop into a worst-case scenario kind of gal as an adult. While parenthood certainly made matters worse, I've been asking, "What if?" for my entire life. I'm pretty much a pro. As a child, I would come up with the craziest hypothetical scenarios and then action plans to accompany them. It happened so often that my family would joke that I'd likely grow up to write a book titled *Rachelle's Book of What-Ifs*. A riveting read I'm sure it would be.

Anyhow, my *what-ifs* come in many shapes and sizes. Sometimes they are full of wishful thinking and hopeful possibility. Other times, however, they are questions riddled with worry and fear. When that's the case—when my hypothesizing goes from having fun to freaking out— I have two choices. I can choose to intentionally move through that worry, or I can stay stuck in it. Trust me, I've never found stuck to be a very effective posture.

When deciding whether to hold on to or let go of our excess material possessions, fear is a monstrosity of a hurdle. We're afraid of regret, inconvenience, financial hardship, wastefulness, and missing out. We worry we'll someday need an item we decluttered or that our once-beloved stuff won't land in the perfect hands. Because of that we hold on just a little longer until we can find the home it deserves. Fear can be paralyzing, causing us to keep clutter even when our rational minds know it's time to let go.

HOW TO FIGHT A CASE OF THE WHAT-IFS

The reality is this: you're going to have to choose between either braving your fear of letting go or settling for the suffocation of a life spent distracted by clutter. Neither path is easy, but only one will lead you off the hamster wheel of clutter maintenance. Here are three strategies to help you choose brave over stuck.

1. Go All In on the What-If

Sometimes it's fear we fear. We avoid addressing what we're worried about, afraid we'll somehow make it worse. I want to give you permission to name exactly what it is you're afraid will happen if you let go of your extras. Go all in on that worst-case scenario and follow your fear to the very end of its story.

If you're prone to collecting clutter because you just can't help but stockpile for the just-in-case, I want you to think through the very worst things that could happen if you do let go. What would you do if you found yourself regretful of having donated something you now need? Let's say you donate those too-small jeans to the thrift store only to finally lose those last few pounds: What would you then do? What if you declutter your game closet only to find yourself sheltered at home again, wishing for a few more board games to keep your family preoccupied? What's the worst thing that could happen if you find yourself up a creek without that Bundt pan?

When I do this, I often find myself laughing after just a few minutes. The further I take my what-ifs, the less power they have over me. I quickly discover just how ridiculous they really are and start to realize just how resourceful I can be when given the opportunity.

2. Remember, You're Resourceful

You, my friend, are a tough cookie. Don't forget that! As you see your fears through to the end, you'll find you have the resourcefulness to figure life out as you go. That worst-case scenario? It's got nothing on you.

The longer you live with less, the more confident and comfortable you'll grow with your very own resourcefulness.

Listen: you're going to borrow a Bundt pan, opt to make a different recipe, or simply use a pan you already have. If you need new jeans after dropping a size, you'll grab a pair from a thrift store, snag your sister's hand-me-downs, or go buy a new pair with all of the money you're saving as a minimalist. The same goes for books, puzzles, and board games: you can swap with friends or neighbors or buy something new for pennies on the dollar at your local thrift store. You'll figure it out; you always have, and you always will. Who knows? Perhaps you'll find the items you gave away are actually items you can do without altogether. (Well, not pants; you do need pants.)

The longer you live with less, the more confident and comfortable you'll grow with your very own resourcefulness.

3. Ask a Different Kind of What-If

Instead of asking, "What if I need this someday?" I want to challenge you to begin to ask a different what-if question—a better one.

"What if someone else needs this right now?"

As I said before, I used to think being a good steward of what I was entrusted with meant holding on to it all for safe keeping. I'd tuck it away for a rainy day, retirement, zombie apocalypse, or you know, a global pandemic. But I had it all wrong. Being a good steward isn't holding on but letting go. It's using what you have, even if that's just five loaves and two fishes (John 6:1–14), to love and serve the person next to you.

SCARCITY

As the world began to shut down during the early months of 2020, people went crazy. Grocery items we had never worried about losing access to started going missing from store shelves. Do you remember feeling even just a little uneasy when you heard your local grocery store was now out of toilet paper? Maybe you didn't run out like a lunatic and fight someone for that last roll. But if you're being honest with yourself, I'm guessing a small part of you thought, "Wait, but what if the world really *does* run out of toilet paper?" We all felt that unease to some degree because it's a natural human response to scarcity.

Scarcity, simply put, is a shortness in supply. When something you need is no longer easily accessible, it can be unnerving. The trouble isn't with our natural desire to secure essentials for our families. That's normal. The problem is that we've been conditioned to respond to scarcity even when the items are inessential or far from scarce. That's what advertisers try to do to us every single day. Companies fabricate scarcity in the form of annual sales, the hottest holiday toy, messages like "only two left in stock," early-bird pricing, and limited editions. All these create within us a sense of urgency. We don't want to miss out, so we make sure to stock up on whatever they're selling, even when we don't really need it. I'm certain that if the media had started pumping out articles about a yarn shortage during the pandemic, everyone would have become devout knitters, scrambling to get their hands on the last ball of yarn.

> *We wake up to what's driving us to consume in the first place and then choose to become more conscious and deliberate consumers of stuff.*

How do we stop letting advertisers bully us out of our lunch money and sucker us into spending what we don't have to buy things we don't even want—let alone truly *need*? We wake up to what's driving us to consume in the first place and then choose to become more conscious and deliberate consumers of stuff. If we don't pay attention, carefully choose, and intentionally decline the message of more, more, more that is playing on loop in the background of everyday life, we don't stand a chance.

ACTUAL SCARCITY

It's important to me that we address the reality that there's a difference between hypothetical what-ifs leading us to hold on *juuust* in case and having firsthand experience with what real scarcity feels like. If you've lived through poverty—or still, today, struggle to make ends meet—the way in which you approach accumulating and decluttering material possessions is going to look much different than it does for someone who has not. Our experiences shape our behavior.

I'm extremely grateful that I'd never spent a day of my life worried about whether I'd have food to eat or access to the groceries our family needed. Because of that, we'd never felt inclined to stock up on backup food or keep a deep freezer full of meat and produce. I'd always just bought what we needed and gone back to the grocery store when we needed more of it.

The COVID-19 pandemic changed that. I've got backups now. I don't know if I'll ever stop keeping backup food from here on out—at least not by choice. I'll keep an extra bag of pancake mix, flour, yeast, frozen chicken, and immunity-support gummy vitamins for my kids (I know, they're probably 90 percent sugar, but they make me feel better). I'm not stocking up out of extreme paranoia—well, maybe a little—but because I know what it feels like to watch the world shut down and need a few things. I want to be prepared if it happens again.

Now, please hear me. This isn't me trying to tell my sob story about the plight of a suburban mom whose grocery store ran out of boneless chicken thighs and toilet paper for a few weeks. I'm simply hoping to acknowledge that letting go of those what-if items isn't always so simple. If you've experienced poverty, ditching some of your backups will be more difficult and perhaps, depending on your current circumstances, not advised. To be in a position to *choose* to live with less is most certainly a privilege. That's what makes the message of messy minimalism so important. It allows you to declutter at the pace of grace while creating a space that serves your real life, whatever those circumstances may be.

MESSY MINIMALIST TIP: BORROW OVER BUY

Instead of immediately hopping online to two-day ship items you need or want, ask around and try to borrow first. When I was growing up, my mother was always sending me across the street to borrow an item or ingredient from our neighbors. Today it's become easier, and sometimes even faster, to order what you need from an online retailer instead of borrowing it. This way of life is only serving to add clutter to our homes and causing us to spend money unnecessarily. Perhaps your sister-in-law has a cake stand or your neighbor can loan you her knitting needles while you give that new hobby a try. Maybe you can let friends borrow your fishing poles for the weekend while you borrow their pasta maker. What can you get away with not actually owning?

7

KNOW THE DRIVING FORCES OF CONSUMERISM

It's not a deal if you don't need it.

—Christine Platt

The question "Why do I want to buy this?" is one I've only started asking myself in recent years. Prior to landing on minimalism, *why* I was feeling inclined to make any particular purchase wasn't even on my radar. If I wanted it, could easily afford it, thought it would bring me joy, or assumed I needed it, I bought it. No questions asked.

Permanently clearing the clutter from your home starts with making better purchasing decisions. We can't do that, however, without understanding what is driving us to consume in the first place. In this chapter we are going to discuss the forces, both external and internal, that drive us to accumulate material possessions.

COMPARISON

We live in one of those subdivisions where a handful of people take lawn care *very* seriously. Us, on the other hand, not so much. We don't chemically treat our lawn or take pride in the mow pattern. While some people look at weeding and gardening as a form of self-care, to us it's more like hard manual labor.

It just so happens that the neighbors who *do* care live directly next door to us. Now, I have no idea what our neighbors *really* think of our lawn. They're far too kind and gracious a folk to ever say a word. However, in the past, when the contrast between our weedy plot of land and their immaculate yard would grow uncomfortably obvious, I'd find my husband out there spraying the lawn. With what? No clue. I'm not even sure it ever made that much of a difference. The only thing we were really hoping for was that our landscape-competent neighbors would see him out there, tilt their heads in sympathy, silently thank us for at least pretending to try, and think to themselves, "Oh, bless their sweet little hearts."

Now that I have kids running around out there barefoot—one fetching sticks with her actual mouth some days—we don't chemically treat our lawn. And it shows.

A couple summers back, my daughter brought it to my attention. She noticed the contrast between our neighbor's dark-green, well-watered, luscious lawn and our sparse, partially brown, weedy one. Except her observation was much different than mine. "I feel so bad for them," she said, pointing toward our neighbors' lawn. "They don't have any flowers in their yard."

The flowers she was referring to, of course, were bright-yellow dandelions. She saw our abundance of weeds as something to be envied.

Comparison is one of the biggest forces driving our overconsumption. We are constantly told that what we have is not enough. We start to think we need to keep up with somebody else's way of life, and we begin looking at our homes, wardrobes, and overall lives as things in need of constant updating. When we've always got one eye on our neighbor's lawn, we run the risk of missing the beauty in our very own.

Now, I'm not suggesting you never replace or repair areas of your home. Our own home could certainly use a flooring face-lift. Our scratched and faded hardwood floors have seen better days. But I'm continuously pushing back the timeline for this undertaking every time I witness one of my children drag a chair across the floor to use as a ladder to reach the Sharpie markers I've strategically hidden on top of the refrigerator. This is why we don't have nice things. I'm simply suggesting that HGTV's number-one goal is to sell you something. That starts by convincing you that your home sucks.

> *We start to think we need to keep up with somebody else's way of life, and we begin looking at our homes, wardrobes, and overall lives as things in need of constant updating.*

I've grown rather fond of my chemical-free weedy lawn, dining table covered in streaks of Sharpie marker, and sparse fireplace mantel— not because they are trending, but because they are mine. I've found no better words within myself than the ones on the pages of *Love Lives Here* by Maria Goff. She says this about comparison: "Go be your family, not someone else's. The thing I'm learning about comparison is that the only way it will leave us alone is if we name it for what is and then ignore it completely. We could spend our time sorting through all of its lies like clothes at a thrift store, or we can spot comparison coming our way, call it a liar, and simply refuse to make eye contact with it."

Rather than letting comparison dictate how you spend your money and cause you to accumulate clutter, choose instead to lean into contentment. You've got an abundance of gifts already planted in your ordinary, messy, everyday life. Stop trying to replicate what it is your neighbor does; instead, turn your attention to the beauty located directly at your very feet.

Besides, the grass will become greener where you water it—or, in our case, where you don't.

CHANGING TRENDS

I've never been described as fashionable. I have, on the other hand, been described as "frumpy." Frumpy, I'm familiar with. Fashionable? Not so much.

When it comes to the latest trends, it seems as though I'm always the last to know. By the time I finally come around to a new trend, odds are good it's already on the way out the door. I'm pretty sure I was the last person in the United States to switch from boot-cut to skinny jeans, and I did so kicking and screaming. Now high-rise jeans are all the rage. At least they are as I write this book. Who knows what will be "in" by the time it's published? I'm sorry, but I just can't shake the mental image of my mom, grandma, and aunts all standing around my grandparents' yellow kitchen in the '80s, drinking coffee with their jeans hiked to the heavens and their shoulder pads standing proud. Here I am, some thirty years later, wearing the very mom jeans I loathed for so long. But as long as shoulder pads don't come back around, I think I'll be okay. That's a trend worth picketing.

> *You've got an abundance of gifts already planted*
> *in your ordinary, messy, everyday life.*

Keeping your wardrobe in style is about as possible as keeping my littlest from making embarrassing remarks in the women's locker room after swim lessons. Not likely. Just when you think you've made it, a confident elderly woman will walk on by in her birthday suit, and all progress will be lost.

Staying trendy is an ever-moving target, always out of reach. And here's the thing: it's designed to be that way. Annie Leonard talks about this concept in her book *The Story of Stuff*. Leonard discusses two concepts contributing to consumerism. We must understand these twin concepts—planned obsolescence and perceived obsolescence—if we want to make better purchasing decisions going forward.

PLANNED OBSOLESCENCE

Have you ever found yourself standing in front of a broken appliance muttering the words, "They don't make 'em like they used to"? Well, it's more than just a cliché. Manufacturers have been designing products to have a shelf life. In *The Story of Stuff*, Leonard says this:

> Producers of Stuff realized that there was an eventual limit to how much people could consume. At some point, everyone would have enough shoes and toasters and cars. At some point, there would be total saturation. And if the factories were going to keep churning out Stuff once consumers were Stuff saturated, then there'd be a glut. And a glut would be very bad for business indeed.
>
> So the architects of the system came up with a strategy to keep consumers buying: planned obsolescence. Another name for planned obsolescence is "designed for the dump."
>
> … In planned obsolescence, products are intended to be thrown away as quickly as possible and then replaced. (That's called "shortening the replacement cycle.")

I can't help but wonder if this is exactly why my grandparents' 1942 Frigidaire refrigerator is still going strong today. It has outlasted the handful of refrigerators my family has owned during my lifetime. I think that refrigerator just may outlive me.

PERCEIVED OBSOLESCENCE

Perceived obsolescence, on the other hand, comes into play every time new fashion trends emerge. It's how the fashion industry remains, well, an industry. Leonard says this:

In this case the item isn't broken, nor is it really obsolete at all; we just perceive it as such. Some people call this "obsolescence of desirability" or "psychological obsolescence." This is where taste and fashion come in to play. The ever-shifting hem lengths of women's skirts and dresses; the chunky heels that are in fashion one season only to be replaced by skinny stilettos the next; the width of men's ties; this year's hot color for cell phones, iPods, toasters, blenders, couches, even kitchen cabinets: this is all perceived obsolescence at work.... Retailers and producers want you to believe that you can't wear the same color or cut from one week to the next and that you'll be less cool, less savvy, and less desirable if you do.

This applies to things like technology, toys, and home decor. Something newer, later, and greater is always on the horizon. Have you ever finished a home renovation project only to think, just a couple years later, that the paint you picked, the chair you chose, or the counters you went with are already out of style?

I don't know about you, but this perceived obsolescence makes me feel played, duped, and manipulated. How is it we've come to believe we're always due something a little newer, a little better? That our favorite rider boots are so 2018? While Americans are spending billions of dollars every year on always-changing trends, they aren't necessarily saving any money either. In fact, 40 percent of Americans don't have a $1,000 emergency fund.

There are a variety of factors that impact a family's ability to save money. Yet keep in mind that companies are paying advertisers good money to convince you that it's more important to be trendy than financially secure.

RETAIL THERAPY

They don't call shopping "retail therapy" for nothing. Buying something new can offer a quick fix—a pick-me-up for feelings of boredom, stress, overwhelm, or low self-esteem. I used to blame my clothes when I didn't feel good about my body. I'd blame my outdated decor for feelings of insecurity and my square footage for the fact that my home was never put together. Instead of addressing the stress, fear, and overwhelm, I'd blame my material possessions for the unrest within me and then set out on a mission to right the wrong, thinking, "A couple new tops oughta do the trick."

Consider whether there are extenuating circumstances in your life driving you to accumulate unnecessarily.

If we aren't confident in who we are or still within our souls, nothing we put on top of our bodies will satisfy. We'll never find peace on a rack at T.J.Maxx, clarity at HomeGoods, or confidence at a blowout bar. Online shopping is just a temporary distraction, not an effective coping strategy. Shopping provides temporary relief, which is exactly why we continually resort to it. But just as fast as the relief rushes in, it's gone again. We're still left feeling empty, seeking something that can't be bought.

We'll talk more about making good purchasing decisions in the next chapter, so I'll just say this. It's important that we take a minute to assess our motivation for purchasing new items before heading to a local retailer or clicking Add to Cart. Pause and pay attention to your stress level. Consider whether there are extenuating circumstances in your life driving you to accumulate unnecessarily.

ACCUMULATION IN THE NAME OF SIMPLICITY

Comparison, changing trends, and a lack of self-awareness aren't the only things keeping us in Camp Consumer. Good intentions will do this as well.

In an attempt to simplify our lives, we can inadvertently do more harm than good, assuming more stuff will lead to simplicity. There is a gadget for just about everything. Meander down the As Seen On TV aisle for a few minutes and you'll see just how far we'll go to simplify our everyday lives. There are gadgets to help us lose weight fast, kitchen appliances to cook meat in record time, and there's even a product to seal a leaky roof without spending time or money on an actual professional. On top of that, we order things like closet systems, sorters, stackable bins, and turntables all in an effort to make our excess stuff more accessible and organized.

It's not all bad. I'm not anti-stuff. Trust me, I still have plenty of it. But let's just take a step back here, blink a couple times, rub the BOGO film from our eyes, and dare to reconsider whether this stuff is *really* making our lives any simpler.

> *You can't buy your way into the simple life. . . . You'll never find simplicity through the practice of more.*

Take my kitchen, for example. I thought all of those gadgets, caddies, slicers, and bowls of varying size were making my life easier. Never did I consider they might be the very things contributing to the chaos. As we decluttered that room, drawer by drawer, I noticed a common theme. We owned multiple items capable of carrying out the same task. Also, it appears we like to slice things. We owned a handheld apple slicer and a vegetable peeler, as well as one of those all-in-one apple slicer / corer / peelers. On top of that, our drawers contained a pizza slicer, an avocado slicer, multiple cheese slicers, as well as a block set of knives. There were probably ten different items in that kitchen all capable of slicing an apple.

Much of what we're buying are items we hope will streamline our homes, offer us freedom from the mundane, and provide us with more time to live the fulfilling lives we desire. With a few exceptions, however, that's rarely how it unfolds. It would always take me forever to find all the pieces to my hand-cranked cheese grater. I'd have to sift through the seven different mixing spoons and five spatulas of varying sizes just to find the handle hiding there, wedged in a web of whisks.

Friend, you can't buy your way into the simple life. There is no such thing as the perfect kitchen gadget, monthly delivery subscription, or storage system that will satisfy your craving for simplicity. You'll never find simplicity through the practice of more.

What's the solution then? How do you push back against these forces of consumerism? You've got to first wake up to which factors are pushing you to overconsume in the first place. Are you driven by comparison? Or perhaps by trying to keep up with changing trends? Do you shop when you're stressed? Or maybe your good intentions to simplify and organize your stuff are actually leading you to accumulate more. Or perhaps, if you're like me, your overconsumption is rooted in a combination of all these driving forces.

We can't fight what we don't see. When you feel the urge to shop, I want you to instead pause and investigate why. What is really at play? Are you looking to numb feelings of overwhelm or worry? Are you hoping to distract yourself from a problem you can't fix? The first step to swimming against the current of overconsumption is to identify what's been dragging you along. The next is to practice the art of conscious consumerism.

MESSY MINIMALIST TIP: CHOOSE ADVENTURE OVER ACCUMULATION

Choosing to push back against the relentless forces of consumerism will be a lifelong undertaking. The advertisements won't end just because you "went minimalist," and the pull to partake will never entirely go away. This must be a decision on your end. Instead of trying to simply strengthen your resolve, make an exchange. Choose to invest in experiences, adventure, and memories over the accumulation of more. Choose a weekend getaway over a high-end handbag. Take a hike with a friend instead of window shopping. Make #experiencesoverthings your mantra. The longer you live into it, the more obvious it will be that making memories trumps buying more stuff, every time.

8

BECOME A MORE
CONSCIOUS CONSUMER

*The goal isn't just to declutter your closet or garage but to
declutter your life. To clear away the myriad of distractions
that ratchet up your anxiety . . . and anesthetize us to what
really matters.*

—John Mark Comer

"Seriously? We need *all* of this?"

"Yes!" I replied with all the confidence in the world. "You're going to
host a party someday, and you'll definitely wish you had these."

About two years prior to my becoming a minimalist, my little brother
and his bride-to-be asked me to join them as they registered for their
upcoming wedding. *Big mistake*. They thought they were taking along

an older, wiser registry guru, since at the time I had ten-plus years of marriage under my belt and all. Instead, they had inadvertently asked along an emergency preparedness expert.

In those days, I operated under the assumption that a wedding gift registry was meant to assist you in stockpiling everything you might need during the entirety of your life span. I mean, what if you end up birthing three sets of twins someday? Surely, you'll wish you'd listened to me and registered for twenty-six bath towels.

Since I had already confiscated the registry gun, my sister-in-law-to-be's protest was in vain. I wandered with them from aisle to aisle, scanning everything I thought they could ever possibly need. Two complete sets of dinner plates? Check! Serving utensils for a party of twenty-four? Check! Backup sheets, multiple-sized mixing bowls, and a cake stand? Check, check, and check. From my recollection, the only item my brother insisted on adding was a quality charcuterie board. A well-stocked and impressive cheese board always has been and always will be a vital component of our family gatherings. (I stand by that today. Long live cheese.)

While they were skeptical of my scan-it-all approach to registering—and rightly so—they assumed I knew what I was doing. After all, older sisters can be pretty convincing.

A CULTURE OF STUFF

It had been quite a few years since I registered for my own wedding. I mean, back then Amazon Prime and smartphones weren't even a thing, at least not in Michigan. Sometimes it feels like the entire Midwest lives beneath a rock. Always the last to know, always the last to catch the wave of new technology. So my experience with creating my own wedding registry had involved asking the advice of everybody I knew and following the expansive registry recommendation list I received from Bed Bath & Beyond.

We invited four hundred people to our wedding. Four hundred! I am Lebanese, so they were practically all family, but still: that's a lot of flipping people. They were an extremely generous crew, and because of that, we received far more gifts than two twentysomethings could ever possibly need.

When my brother and sister-to-be asked me what to register for, I offered them the same advice that was offered to me: All. The. Things. Never mind the fact that ten years later I still had a stash of unused wedding gifts stockpiled in my basement. It's embarrassing to admit, but our home was stuffed full, and we were absolutely clueless to the fact that perhaps this wasn't how we were meant to be living.

Based on the statistics, we weren't the only ones who drank the Kool-Aid of overconsumption. Here are some facts showing how far from alone we were:

- Inside the average American home you'll find roughly three hundred thousand items.
- Only 3.7 percent of the world's children live in the United States, yet our children own 47 percent of the world's toys and children's books.
- Since the 1950s, the average home in the United States has more than doubled in size.
- The self-storage industry in the United States has grown at a faster rate than the US population.
- In 2018, textiles made up 7.7 percent of the 11.3 million US tons of municipal solid waste generated.
- On average, Americans each throw away 70 pounds of clothing and textiles per year.

So you can imagine how annoyed my brother and his wife were when, one year after their wedding, I proclaimed myself a minimalist. My notoriously kind and reserved sister-in-law piped right up. "Excuse me!" she said. "You just forced me to register for a cake stand I didn't even want. *Now* you go minimalist?"

"Yeeaahh," I said. "About that—sorry. I was totally wrong."

SPENDING FREEZE

I can still remember my husband's face when he arrived home from work on day one of my minimalist journey. It would still be a couple weeks before he began his own. Hesitantly he entered our bedroom, scanning the mountains of clothes I intended to ditch. He nodded, not saying a word as I took him for a tour, pointing out which piles were going to my sisters, which items I was donating to the rescue mission, and which stuff just needed to be trashed.

Finally I led him to our closet, face-to-face with a heaping pile of shoes I wanted to let go of.

That's when he spoke up. "But wait. Hold on. Are you going to just end up buying a bunch of new shoes to replace all of these?"

It was a legitimate question. One that needed to be addressed. With it, I knew exactly what our next step needed to be. A spending freeze. A big one. Not forever, but for now. Not only did my spending habits need a major detox, but I needed to prove to myself, as well as to my husband, that I was committed to this life of less for good.

So that day I halted any and all miscellaneous spending for two months. We bought nothing that wasn't absolutely essential. We cut out everything from home decor, gadgets, and new clothes to lattes, eating out, and even snack foods like tortilla chips. If we didn't need it to survive, we didn't buy it.

Soon—and it's amazing how fast you start to notice this—on top of letting go of more stuff than we were bringing in, we were also saving more money than ever before. Bonus!

> *I knew exactly what our next step needed to be. A spending freeze. A big one. Not forever, but for now.*

Let me make this very clear. It does not matter how much you get rid of if you don't also stop the flow of material items into your home. It's as simple as that. If you don't stop buying excess stuff, you're never going to find yourself living uncluttered. It's basic math.

A spending freeze is a critical first step in both shifting the way you view the accumulation of material possessions and in cultivating a minimalist mindset. The spending freeze doesn't have to last forever, but it will provide you with an aerial view of how you're spending your money and ultimately your time. Money doesn't grow on trees. (Trust me, my kids bought me a potted plant called a "money tree" for Christmas a few years ago. It sat on my mantel for a good year before succumbing to its inevitable demise, and nothing.)

Instead, we must head off to work, spending much of our lives at jobs we either love, tolerate, or completely despise, in an effort to pay for these things that make up our lives. At the end of the day, we should be proud of the items we spend our money on; after all, we are using the nonrenewable resource of time to gather them.

THE WASTEFULNESS OF FRUGALITY

You may be thinking to yourself, "Oh, this spending freeze thing doesn't really apply to me because I'm not a big spender. I'm already a really frugal person." I'd like to take a moment to challenge this line of thinking. Frugal people can be just as wasteful as shopaholics.

My husband, Paul, is one of the most frugal men I know, second only to my very own father. I grew up watching my dad eat food *well* beyond the "best by" date—you know, to get his money's worth. I'm talking dangerously beyond the point when it should have been ingested by a human. He still prides himself on it today.

Don't be deceived, though. Frugality does not necessarily make you a conscious consumer. In fact, if you aren't careful, frugality puts you at an even greater risk of wasteful spending. My husband would only buy clothing he found on the clearance rack at an outlet store. Noble, right? But if you took a closer look, you'd see he wasted tons of money on low-quality clothing. Blinded by his own frugality, he loved the feeling of walking away with an overstuffed bag of items totaling less than thirty dollars. Never mind that the jeans weren't the right size or the sleeves of that sweater were too short. He knew full well that it would only take one run through the dryer for some of those tops to be deemed unwearable. He didn't care. If it was $6.98, Paul was buying it.

Like many of us, Paul justified these types of purchases with comments like, "Well, it's such a great price. Even if I only get a few wears out of it, it will be worth it."

These items never lasted very long, but they did a fantastic job of cluttering up our closet. Frugal people also tend to refuse to let go of anything, thus creating a cycle of buying low-quality items, replacing those low-quality items with more low-quality items, and then holding on to all of it, forever, amen.

Don't get me wrong: frugality can be a fantastic thing when practiced wisely. And I'm not suggesting you spend exorbitant amounts of money on high-end, name-brand pieces. This isn't about swinging to the polar opposite end of the spectrum here. I'm saying we should simply be looking for quality over quantity. That may mean you still hit up garage sales, thrift stores, and outlet malls, but instead of buying all the things, you get pickier. Look for brands notorious for high quality, with a reputation of durability. Be willing to own fewer articles of clothing that may cost a little more instead of living with a closet jam-packed full of discount clothing.

> *Frugality does not necessarily make you a conscious consumer. In fact, if you aren't careful, frugality puts you at an even greater risk of wasteful spending.*

Paul eventually came around, and he has since begun buying with much greater intention. He is still the same frugal man I married. He's simply exchanged his thirty stretched-out cheap T-shirts for just a handful of higher-quality ones he loves. Trust me, he'll always check out the clearance section first, but now he's willing to walk away empty handed.

No matter whether you call yourself frugal or spendy, I highly recommend you start your messy minimalist journey with a spending freeze. They say it takes twenty-eight days to develop a new habit. I'd recommend at least forty days for good measure. If you happen to have a spendthrift significant other putting up a fight, see if you can compromise with an incentive. Come up with a goal. Perhaps you can spend that time paying off debt, saving for a big-ticket item, or going out on a more extravagant date night. If they are still hesitant, well, you just do you. Halt your own spending, then slowly ease back in, buying what you really need with greater intention.

HOW TO MAKE PURCHASES LIKE A MESSY MINIMALIST

Becoming a more conscious consumer takes practice, especially when you've spent decades of your life practically sleepwalking while shopping. A conscious consumer is someone who is awake, aware, and intentional about their purchases. They don't buy on a whim or easily succumb to the lure of advertisements. This may mean you are buying fewer items, higher-quality items, more environmentally friendly items, or simply buying local. However you opt to consciously consume, one thing is consistent: you're conscious while consuming. You're paying attention to your spending rather than simply doing what you've always done before. Here are five tips to help you make purchases like a messy minimalist.

1. Try to Go Without

Conscious consumers pause before replacing an item. Just because something breaks doesn't mean it must be replaced immediately. It certainly might need to be replaced, but not necessarily. Look around and get creative. Perhaps you already have an item that can do the trick. Or maybe you're moving into a new season of life and can simply let go of that thing altogether. Make it a rule to never buy an item on an impulse. Instead, give yourself the time to pause. During that pause, ask yourself questions, such as:

- Do I really need it?
- Do I have something that can perform the same task?

- Can I do without it?
- Do I love it?
- Am I just replacing it because I've always owned it?
- Does it serve the life I'm trying to live?
- Do I just think I need it because everybody else has one?
- Will it force me to buy even more things I don't really need?

As conscious consumers, we are willing to get uncomfortable and reevaluate the way we spend. We push back against those driving forces of consumerism, and we check ourselves when we find we're buying an item for the wrong reason. This is a lifelong process, one we'll need to practice diligently every day.

A conscious consumer is someone who is awake, aware, and intentional about their purchases.

To this day, if I'm not paying careful attention, I'll find myself browsing online during times of increased stress. It's important that we train our brains to first attempt to do without. This way, we can buy ourselves enough time to first do that inner work and evaluate whether an item is worth buying at all.

2. Choose Quality over Quantity

I'd rather own thirty quality articles of clothing than three hundred low-quality items that will need replacing every few months. When I say low quality, I'm not just referring to the price tag. We can find both quality pieces *and* junk on the shelves of box stores and trendy high-end boutiques alike. One of my favorite shirts right now is an eight-dollar T-shirt from Target. It goes with everything, washes well, and fits me just right.

Sometimes, however, choosing quality does mean we spend a bit more money—not to keep up an image but because we want our winter boots to last a long time, our tees to not become crop tops, and our dinnerware to be able to withstand the toddler years. Choosing higher-quality products can help us get the biggest bang for our buck.

3. When Possible, Buy Used

Secondhand stores and garage sales are a great place to look for items you may need. Thrifting is my favorite way to buy. It's like a treasure hunt that usually ends in me saving money. On top of that, I'm giving stuff a second life while avoiding adding more clutter to the earth. I've found things like a bento box for my daughter's lunch box for a dollar, an almost-new lawn mower for just eighty bucks, and board games for next to nothing. Up until now, most of my kids' clothes have come from mom-to-mom and garage sales. (The older they get, the more challenging it has become.)

4. Let Go of the Desire to Own All the Beauty You See

You don't need to personally own every beautiful thing within arm's reach. Advertisers would certainly have you believe otherwise, but it's perfectly acceptable to admire beautiful things from a distance. They can still add value to your life without also becoming your own personal property. Not every adorable top, cozy rug, or beautiful work of art you happen upon needs to take up residence in your home. It's okay to simply admire your friend's jacket, your brother's gorgeous kitchen, or your neighbor's lush, green lawn. It does not have to become yours as well.

5. Make Generosity a Priority

A minimalist state of mind is a generous one. To be fully conscious in our consumption means considering ways in which we can make *generosity* a priority. In his book *How to Be Rich*, Andy Stanley writes, "Whenever we have more than we need, our natural assumption will be that it's for our own consumption." When cutting back on the mindless spending, consider people, organizations, and causes you can shift some of your resources toward. As you declutter your home from top to bottom, don't be surprised if you find more joy in generosity than you ever did in the accumulation of more.

MESSY MINIMALIST TIP: BE PREPARED TO GET IT WRONG

Making purchases as a conscious consumer will come with a lot of trial and error. As messy minimalists, we give ourselves the same grace when making purchases as we do when letting go. Don't forget that you're up against a gazillion-dollar advertising industry, working overtime to sell you the things you need as well as the things you don't. We've gone from seeing five hundred advertisements a day back in the 1970s to up to five thousand today. New trends pop up daily, and with social media influencers, algorithms, and cookies all working against us, the onslaught is endless.

Know this: you're going to get it wrong. You're going to end up purchasing something you wish you hadn't. I've done it, and you will too. However, with messy minimalism as our guardrail, we can quickly veer back on track, knowing we don't actually have to keep that itchy scarf until the end of time.

9

REDUCE DECISION FATIGUE

Creating routines that require little to no decision making is a daily act of self-compassion.

—Lisa Avellan

One July evening, my husband and I found ourselves on vacation, roaming the streets of Barcelona kid-free and with nowhere to be. It was fantastic. Dinnertime was approaching—well, *our* dinnertime was approaching. People in Spain eat dinner at about the same time US midwesterners like me are crawling into bed. In the spirit of soaking up that Spanish culture, we gave it our all and waited to eat dinner as late as humanly possible. Now we were ravenous.

We didn't have a plan in place, but there were restaurants everywhere. I mean, how hard could it be to find a place to eat, right? Using the

Tripadvisor app on his phone, my husband began to look over the menus and read reviews for the restaurants nearest us. I helped by hovering over his shoulder and nixing his recommendations. We took turns with the phone, slowly widening our view on the map until deciding on a restaurant a good distance away.

We walked for a while, growing both hangrier and more annoyed with each other by the minute. Eventually we arrived at our restaurant of choice. It was closed. Of course.

This happened a number of times before we finally gave up on the idea of eating somewhere *perfect* and opted for the restaurant directly in front of us. I mean, by this point our marriage practically depended on it.

We left Barcelona a few days later and traveled to the small town of Tamariu, on the southern end of the Costa Brava. It. Was. Stunning. This small town had just a few restaurants to choose from, most boasting their own gorgeous view of the Mediterranean Sea. Deciding where to eat each night was a piece of cake. Perhaps it was the sea air or the abundance of local cava, but we never argued over where to eat. With just a few great options available to us, deciding took minutes.

I wish I could say our experience in Barcelona was the first indecision-induced restaurant conflict we'd ever experienced, but that wasn't our first rodeo. It's played out the same exact way from San Francisco to Miami and from Paris to New Orleans. Even in our own hometown, we've struggled to decide on a place to chew food when there are too many great options to choose from.

Yes, this *is* what you call a first-world problem. But it's also a result of what is known as *decision fatigue*. Decision fatigue occurs when we become overwhelmed by either the sheer number of decisions we have to make in a given day or the abundance of options available to us. It can happen at home, at work, when selecting our groceries, or even on a supposedly stress-free vacation.

When this happens—when I become overwhelmed by either choices or decisions—I tend to stick my head in the sand and ignore everything.

I stop answering my phone and replying to messages. I refuse to make a single decision and procrastinate on both big and small tasks. I know, just call me Superwoman. If you've ever felt crippled by the number of decisions to make in a day and the number of choices available to you, or if you've ever spiraled down the wormhole of reading product review after product review hoping to find the perfect option, it's likely you were suffering from decision fatigue.

JAM STUDY

In 2000 Sheena Iyengar, psychologist and author of *The Art of Choosing*, published findings from a study conducted at a local upscale grocery store known for its wide variety of options. I'm talking 150 kinds of vinegar and more than 250 types of cheeses. Iyengar and the store owner were hoping to learn whether or not more options actually resulted in more sales.

In this study, Iyengar and her assistants set up sample tables of jam on two separate Saturdays. Every hour, they rotated the number of different sample flavors being offered: providing either twenty-four flavors to taste test or just six. They found that while 60 percent of passersby stopped at the table when they were displaying twenty-four sample flavors (as opposed to 40 percent when the display contained just six), they neither tasted nor purchased more jam. In fact, 30 percent of those who tasted jam when the table held fewer options bought a jar, while just 3 percent bought a jar after tasting from the table with twenty-four sample flavors. While more options were initially attractive, ultimately, they resulted in far fewer purchases.

Iyengar further explains that the jam was not available for purchase at the sample tables themselves. After tasting the jam, participants wanting to buy a jar had to meander to the jam aisle, make their final selection, and then purchase the jam. Those who visited the aisle after stopping at the sample table when it had *fewer jam options* were observed confidently making their jam selection and leaving the aisle. People who had stopped at the table when it had *more* options continued to hem and haw as they were presented with an even greater selection within the aisle, and many eventually walked away empty handed.

"When the options are few, we can be happy with what we choose since we are confident that it is the best possible choice for us," writes Iyengar. "When the options are practically infinite, though, we believe that the perfect choice for us must be out there somewhere and that it's our responsibility to find it."

Iyengar found similar results in a later study with the Vanguard Group, which was interested in learning more about participation rates in their retirement plans. "What we found was that as plans offered people more options, participation rates dropped," Iyengar says. "And so the more choices you gave people the lower the participation rates.... When we looked at people who actually did participate, who actually made the choice, even there we found that giving people more choices didn't actually make them better choosers. It turned out that the more choices we gave them, the more likely they were to avoid investing in equities and put more of their money in bonds and money markets."

In other words: not only are we less likely to make a decision when faced with too many options; when we *do* decide, we don't necessarily decide well.

Did you know we make upward of thirty-five thousand decisions a day? When I first read that number, it sounded like an exaggeration to me. Really? Thirty-five *thousand*? The more I thought about it, though, the more it seemed possible. From the moment our eyes open in the morning, we're making decisions. Do I get up or hit snooze? Should I have a sip of water or make a beeline for the coffee pot? Which mug do I want to use today? Will I work out this morning? Should I wipe up that spilled coffee now or deal with it later? Should I respond to these emails now or later? Can I make it back upstairs to drink this coffee in silence before the kids start asking for breakfast?

That's just within a couple minutes of getting out of bed and only involves the decisions we're consciously making on behalf of ourselves.

Add in the decisions we make on the job or on behalf of our family—well, by the time dinner rolls around, many of us are ready to stop thinking altogether. It's not just grand, life-altering decisions depleting our internal reservoir. It's those little ones too. The everyday questions like, What's for dinner? Which route should I take to work? Did you call the plumber yet? Mom, can I have a snack? Can you stop off for milk on your way home from work? What time works best for a meeting?

Not only are we less likely to make a decision when faced with too many options; when we do *decide, we don't necessarily decide well.*

Sound familiar? Sheesh, I'm tired just having written that because I've *totally* been putting off calling the plumber.

The numbers are a bit irrelevant anyway. Whether you literally make 35,000 or just 3,500 decisions in a given day, the reality is this: by the end of the day, it often feels like we've made a million.

So what's the solution? How do we combat decision fatigue like a messy minimalist? Intentional simplicity.

INTENTIONAL SIMPLICITY

Intentional simplicity is the act of purposefully simplifying specific areas of your life to reduce the number of necessary decisions and invest your best self where it matters most. It's choosing to streamline mundane decisions in order to reserve mental energy for more important endeavors throughout the day.

The term *decision fatigue* was first coined by social psychologist Roy F. Baumeister. According to an article in the *New York Times Magazine*, Baumeister's research shows that "people with the best self-control are the ones who structure their lives so as to conserve willpower. They don't schedule endless back-to-back meetings. They avoid temptations like all-you-can-eat buffets, and they establish habits that eliminate the mental effort of making choices. Instead of deciding every morning whether or not to force themselves to exercise, they set up regular appointments to work out with a friend. Instead of counting on willpower to remain robust all day, they conserve it so that it's available for emergencies and important decisions."

This is exactly why I choose to keep a simplified wardrobe. We'll get to the how behind simplifying your closet in a few chapters, but I'm not alone in purposefully reducing the number of articles of clothing I wear. Melissa Coleman, author of *The Minimalist Kitchen*, opts to wear a simple, adorable uniform. Christine Platt, author of *The Afrominimalist's Guide to Living with Less*, keeps a vibrant yet minimalist wardrobe. And Simple Families founder Denaye Barahona, author of *Simple Happy Parenting*, ruthlessly decluttered her closet years ago and today keeps a tiny wardrobe. Even Barack Obama limits the number of clothes he has to choose from. Back in 2012, he told reporter Michael Lewis why, as president, he wore only gray or blue suits: "I'm trying to pare down decisions. I don't want to make decisions about what I'm eating or wearing. Because I have too many other decisions to make." Every single one of them has found that limiting the number of clothing items they have to choose from each morning leaves them with a greater capacity for more important matters.

Simplifying our wardrobes is just one of the many ways we can implement intentional simplicity. Grocery shopping and meal planning is another. When our family underwent that major spending freeze during the first few months of our minimalist journey, we also began grocery shopping at Aldi. During my first trip, I was confident that I'd spend less money on our groceries that week, but I had no idea how much mental energy I'd save as well. At Aldi, you won't find entire aisles dedicated to bread, fruit snacks, or granola bars. The options aren't endless. Getting through the grocery store takes a fraction of the time, and you may find yourself better able to resist the pressure to impulse shop. (Outside the cheese aisle, that is. Cranberry-coated goat cheese for $2.99? Yes please!)

We no longer solely get our groceries at Aldi, mainly because my kids consume fruits and veggies like they're baby hippos. I started buying our produce in bulk to try and keep up. Yet the habits I developed when shopping with fewer choices remain and have informed the simple way I plan meals for our family to this day. Instead of a detailed, monthlong, impossible-to-maintain meal plan, we started a simple meal rotation system. I decide on three or *maybe* four meals for the month and rotate through them over and over and over. Occasionally we'll change up the side dishes depending on what's in season or order take out, but I keep our main meals the same.

> *With every corner of your life you intentionally simplify, you'll discover a little more left in the tank at the end of each day.*

Yes, on and off, for the better part of the last three years, with the occasional exception, the Crawfords have had tacos, roasted chicken, and spaghetti every single week. This simple meal rotation causes us to waste less food, saves us both time and money grocery shopping, and has eliminated the last-minute, four o'clock in the afternoon panic of, "Crap! What am I going to feed these people?" I'd be perfectly content having popcorn, a cheese stick, and a glass of wine for dinner. But our pediatrician and the judicial system wouldn't be too pleased if that's what I served my children as well.

With every corner of your life you intentionally simplify, you'll discover a little more left in the tank at the end of each day. What you decide to do with that newfound energy is up to you.

People are always asking me where I found the time to write a book, especially while home with three kids during a global pandemic. Yeah, sure, maybe I forgot it was bath night more often than normal and called cheese sticks and Go-Gurt "lunch" a few too many times. But I've found intentional simplicity to be the path to productivity. It's the secret doorway most people miss.

MESSY MINIMALIST TIP:
CREATE A SIMPLE MORNING ROUTINE

A simple morning routine will reduce decision fatigue right out of the gate and give your brain a bit of a head start for the day. Wake up at the same time each day. Eat the same thing for breakfast every morning. Pack your kids the exact same lunch every day. Trust me, they'll live.

10

STOP CHASING ORGANIZATION

If organizing your stuff worked, you'd be organized by now.
—Courtney Carver

Just in case my enthusiasm for minimalism has started to take the shape of a high horse, I want to make one thing very, very clear. I *like* stuff. I *have* stuff. *Lots* of it. I own an air popper, an outdoor grill, and a cottage. I have a coffee pot, a blow dryer, and a full set of dishes. There's none of that "one plate per person" stuff going on up in here. I love my dishwasher, washing machine, and rely heavily on my air conditioner in the summertime and my heated blanket in the winter.

Rest assured that if you decide this messy minimalism thing is for you, there isn't a membership class. You won't be handed a list of items you're not allowed to own. You don't need to sell your skis (assuming you actually use them) nor even your cottage in order to buy into what messy minimalism has to offer. You still get to own stuff. The difference is that now the stuff you own actually adds value to your life rather than distracting you from it.

The point of messy minimalism isn't to eliminate every item until eventually you're living in an ice-cold cubicle with just a pallet to sleep on and a sheet for warmth. Then again, if that's your dream, you do you.

> *Trust me: I'm not here to take your stuff. I'm just here to offer a new way to look at it.*

Eliminating the extras, the excess, and the clutter only accentuates our favorite things. Go ahead and indulge your scrapbooking obsession, bake your heart out, knit your weekends away, and kayak until the cows come home. Our goal is to make more time to spend on those things. Trust me: I'm not here to take your stuff. I'm just here to offer a new way to look at it.

CHASING ORGANIZATION

My guess is that we've got a lot in common, especially if you've stuck with me this far. Maybe you're a little less messy than I am or don't feel so opinionated on the subject of cheese. I'm sure you've never lost your child's car seat by accidentally buckling it into a stranger's vehicle (#itsfine). Odds are good, though, that you, too, have wasted a fair amount of time on the wrong things.

For me, one of the biggest time wasters has been chasing organization.

"This weekend we are going to organize the basement!"
"This morning I'm going to organize the toys."
"We've got to get the garage in order."
"Check out what I did in the pantry. It's soooo organized now."

Each of those sentences have flowed through my lips on numerous occasions.

The thought of everything in our homes being perfectly sorted and placed into designated bins, cubbies, shelves, or baskets is alluring. I tried and failed for years, buying shelving and bins from IKEA and totes and baskets from HomeGoods. I figured if I could only get the right *system* in place, then maybe, just maybe, I could keep this home of ours in order. At one time we owned three separate toy shelves, all strategically located in different areas of our home, each cubby meant for a specific type of toy: Hot Wheels, Fisher-Price Little People, Star Wars action figures, Transformers, Disney Princess dolls, and LEGO bricks were each assigned their own corner of my real estate.

The problem was that the little hands I placed in charge of putting these toys away never managed to "get" my system. I mean, let's be honest, they hardly tried. I can't say I blame them, though. It was just too much to manage. So who was it that wound up spending Saturday morning shuffling plastic junk from one bin to another, redoing their insufficient attempt at putting everything away? Not my children. No, it was me, once again using my down time to try to organize our excess stuff. All to watch them undo my careful organization in an instant.

You do not need more bins; you need less stuff.

This cycle went on for years, and I never once stopped to question the chaotic and cluttered life we were living. I always assumed the problem was too few bins, unbearably stubborn children, or my own incompetence.

If you've found yourself stuck in the crazy cycle of organization, consider this your wake-up call. Stop it. Just stop. Those areas in your home prone to clutter? They don't need to be rearranged or organized; they need to be pruned. Something has to go.

You do not need more bins; you need less stuff. There is rarely an organizational problem that can't be solved by owning *less*. From toys and T-shirts to bedsheets and kitchen towels. I'm living proof of this important truth. Owning less is the secret to finally getting organized.

TURN OFF THE WATER

We've owned a cottage on a lake since our kids were just babies. Long before minimalism was ever on our radar. To this day we love spending as much time there as possible, and minimalism has done nothing but give us more time to do exactly that. Year after year, it continues to be a place that brings us closer together and adds joy to our lives. Except for that one winter, when it flooded.

We had just spent the previous summer renovating the kitchen. It was one of the many rooms of our fixer-upper in need of some serious work. We gutted it from top to bottom, ripping down a wall of cabinetry, creating as much counterspace as we could in this tiny cottage kitchen, and of course, adding a dishwasher. (Why do so many of my stories involve a dishwasher?)

Anyway, we had planned on visiting our cottage during the winter months, but it never happened. Between our oldest starting kindergarten, subzero Michigan weather, and life in general, we never made it out there. Around early March we decided to take a trip to the lake to, you know, "check on it." When we arrived, I hopped out, leaving Paul to unbuckle the kiddos, and went to unlock the front door. Before I even opened the door, I knew. I could smell it.

There was water everywhere, and a steady stream still spraying out from beneath that new kitchen sink. I frantically—which is a grossly underexaggerated way to describe my panic—yelled to Paul. I have no clue what he did after that or where our children even were because I was on a mission to find a bucket to catch the water. Yes, you read that right. A bucket. I panicked.

I headed to our garage, running through knee-deep snow, in search of this bucket that I had, for some ridiculous reason, made a priority. Maybe

I thought it would magically turn back time? I don't know. The garage, of course, was locked, but that didn't stop me from trying to get in. I kicked at the door, hoping to knock it down. I was solely, and irrationally, committed to finding a bucket to solve our flood problem.

As you might imagine, kicking down a door is much more difficult than they make it look like in the movies, and this door wouldn't give. I then spotted a flower planter on my neighbor's porch. They, too, were gone for the winter, but I remember thinking, "They'll totally understand why I stole their planter when they come back in the summer." After making my way through the snow, again, I tried to lift that planter to dump out its frozen contents onto their porch. Like a good neighbor. But the planter wouldn't budge either. Turns out it was made of cement.

I scurried back over toward our front porch, shouting to Paul, "I can't find a bucket!" To which he responded, "We don't need a bucket! We need to figure out how to turn the water off."

Eventually we found the water valve hidden beneath the floor of the new kitchen cabinet, as well as the culprit of the leak: a faulty dishwasher valve.

> *No amount of decluttering will ever result in a*
> *cleared-out home if you keep bringing in stuff.*

Our efforts to organize are often much like my sad attempt to find a bucket. More than one hundred thousand gallons of water had been spraying into our home for weeks. Sure, a bucket would have made me feel better in that moment, but it wasn't a solution. We needed to stop the flow of water *into* our home before cleanup could occur.

No amount of decluttering will ever result in a cleared-out home if you keep bringing in stuff. And that goes for organizational supplies as well. Totes, shelving, toy bins, and buckets aren't a long-term solution. In the spirit of tough love, I'll say this: If you're not going to change the way you purchase and accumulate going forward, why even bother with decluttering? It might scratch the itch of that habitual cycle of organization. But if you want less clutter tomorrow and the next day and the next—if you want to stop organizing and reorganizing and then organizing again—stop bringing stuff in. You don't need a bucket! You need to turn the water off.

TO MOVE OR NOT TO MOVE

A few years ago, we seriously considered moving. The year before we found minimalism, we had gone from toying with the idea of moving to figuring it must be time because we had "outgrown our space." Like many other Americans, we assumed more space and a bigger place were our only options.

Deep down, though, neither Paul or I really wanted to leave this home. You see, my dad is a builder, and together we had helped him to build this house. I had laid insulation during the day and headed to work to deliver babies at night. We had helped our electrician friend run the electrical lines, and we had painted every wall and filled every nail hole. (For the record, there are a bazillion nail holes in the trim of a new home. The more time I spent filling them, the sloppier my work became. It shows to this day.)

> *If you want a more organized home, begin by*
> *shutting off the flow of material items into it.*

We've got our blood, sweat, and tears in the very floorboards around here, which is exactly why we dragged our feet in regard to moving. Maybe we could add another garage stall instead? Or extra cabinetry to the kitchen? Neither of us really wanted to move. We just needed more space for all our stuff.

Thankfully we found minimalism in the nick of time and took moving off the table. Turns out we didn't need more space after all; we just needed to ditch some things. Lots of things! I can't say we'll *never* move, but I can promise you this: we'll never move to make space for more stuff.

Finishing a basement, moving into a larger home, adding on or customizing closets: these upgrades won't solve an underlying too-much-stuff problem. They may help contain the disaster for a little a while. But if you haven't turned off the water, it won't be long before you're outside, knee-deep in snow, trying to steal your neighbor's planter.

If you want a more organized home, begin by shutting off the flow of material items into it. Once you've stopped the rising waters, you can begin to effectively let go of the items cluttering your home in the first place.

It's then that everything important will find a place.

MESSY MINIMALIST TIP: THE TEN-MINUTE TIDY

Even when everything has a place, someone still has to be responsible for putting it where it goes. In a home full of messy people, that's the most difficult part of all of this. The actually putting something away part. Even after you've minimized your possessions, when everything you own is sprawled across the floor, it will still feel like chaos. In those moments, I remind myself that minimalism doesn't mean always tidy; it just means easily tidied. And then I call for a ten-minute tidy.

We usually do this before our kids go to bed, but from time to time I'll shout it out in the middle of the day. When my children hear me say, "Ten-minute tidy!" they hop up with smiles on their faces and scramble as fast as they can to put their things away. Bahahaha. Wouldn't that be nice? No, they still turn into zombie-sloth children with the muscle mass of a pencil. Apparently everything they own goes from weighing next to nothing to a million pounds. Ten minutes occasionally turns into twenty-five, but still, it gets the job done.

11

STOP CHASING PERFECTION

Perfection is a poison that pretends to be a vitamin.

—Jon Acuff

I can't tell you the number of times I've been asked the most complicated decluttering questions by people who have yet to declutter one single area of their home. They're intrigued by the idea of intentionally living with less. But their minds then immediately jump to the hardest parts.

They ask questions such as these:

"Yeah, but how am I going to get my kids on board?"
"What am I going to do about our storage unit?"
"What about my family photos?"

"My grandmother passed down her china to me. I don't use it, but I
could never get rid of it."

Instead of effecting change in the simpler areas of their home first,
they head right on over to the record collection they inherited from their
favorite uncle, point to it, and say, "See? What about these? Eh? What
do you expect me to do with *these*?" As if they've just proved minimalism
could never possibly work for them.

Finding answers to questions such as these is certainly important . . .
eventually. But beginning the decluttering process with the hardest parts
first is a minimalist death trap. It's guaranteed to leave you stuck right out
of the gate.

Messy minimalism isn't all or nothing. Stop
asking the hard questions first.

Let me ask you this: Say you were to never get around to decluttering
your paper situation, a single family photo, or that beloved record
collection. But instead, you simply went all in on every not-so-
sentimental area of your home. Would you be better off? Would your
home be a more peaceful environment? Would you be able to get
dressed with less stress, tidy up more quickly, and find your favorite
things more easily? I'm confident the answer is yes.

I'm certainly not telling you to never tackle those hard areas. I *am*,
however, saying that even if you never do, it's okay. Messy minimalism
isn't all or nothing. Stop asking the hard questions first. Walk on over to
your linen closet and get rid of half of your bath towels. Boom! Day
one: done.

Let this life of less transform your day-to-day life and then, from
there, decide how far you want to take it.

If your mind keeps going to the hardest parts first, stop and ask
yourself: Why? What's really going on here? If minimalism isn't for you,
that's fine. No hard feelings. I'll try to get over it. But if you truly believe

it could change your life, then why do you insist on going to the hardest parts first?

I've got a guess.

PERFECTIONISM

I've noticed a similarity among those who struggle to get started with minimalism and those who continually find themselves distracted by all of those seemingly impossible-to-declutter areas—or those who struggle with both. The problem often has less to do with our sentimental attachments or the effort required and more to do with our desire to want it done perfectly—and, like, yesterday. Basically, we are all a bunch of impatient perfectionists.

Consider this scenario: Jen has a conversation with a friend committed to minimalism, and she comes to realize that her own excess stuff is the cause of her relentless sense of overwhelm. Jen gets excited and thinks, "Time to begin! It's all gotta go!" When Jen arrives home she wanders around, contemplating where to begin. She *really* wants to head straight for her kids' toys, but she's confident there will be a mutiny if she does. Besides, she knows it's important to model minimalism, so she should go first.

The kitchen could sure use a declutter, but Jen doesn't think she has the time to tackle that today. Besides, she needs to make some room in the pantry before she can really let go and move stuff around in the kitchen. Jen heads to her wardrobe, then hesitates. She has been meaning to lose a few pounds, and she certainly doesn't want to let go of her smaller-sized clothing, just in case. She sifts through a couple drawers and finds a few items she knows she doesn't need. But then she remembers how much money they cost her. "Should I try to sell them?" Jen asks herself. And then, "Where would be the best place to sell these?" Better to hang on to them, she concludes, until she figures that out.

She decides to move on to decluttering her linen closet, but when she opens the door, she finds an overflowing number of random items.

Jen then recalls a few beautiful linen closet storage systems she saw on Pinterest, so she decides to go online to order some bins and matching hanging sorters first. "I'll be able to *really* declutter this if I have the right system in place," she thinks.

After thirty minutes of scrolling, Jen notices the time and realizes she has to go get her kids from school. "Ugh! I don't have time for this decluttering thing," she thinks as she grabs her keys and heads out the door.

Sound at all familiar?

At first glance, Jen may appear to be overwhelmed, facing limitations on her time, or simply incapable of really focusing. While those may sometimes be true, I've found these factors aren't often the *real* problem for people struggling to get started minimizing. The bigger problem is that Jen is actually struggling with perfectionism. She can't seem to settle for good enough, for now. If Jen can't do it perfectly, then she isn't going to do it at all.

Given my claim of being a messy person, you might be surprised to know that I also struggle with perfectionism. It may seem like a perfectionist would be the kind of person who kept everything perfectly in order. But that's just one side of the coin. Yes, some perfectionists are good at perfection; but those of us who know we'll never be able to meet our own unrealistic exceptions opt to not even try. If it can't look perfect, I'll just stick my head in the sand and avoid it altogether.

Jon Acuff says it well in his book, *Finish*: "Perfectionism trots out a laundry list of reasons you shouldn't begin. . . . If you ignore this initial barrage and start something, perfectionism changes its tune completely. Now it says that you have to do it perfectly. It's the only possibility that is acceptable."

THREE WAYS TO FIGHT PERFECTIONISM AND JUST GET STARTED

Maybe you're having a hard time getting started on the minimalist journey. Or maybe you find yourself overwhelmed at the thought of decluttering your family photos when you've got a mountain of tattered sheets and bath products lingering in your closets. If you are struggling with perfectionism—whatever that looks like for you—here are a few tips to help.

1. Don't Get Caught Up in Comparison

Comparison causes us to feel stuck even before we've gotten started. It shuts down creativity and turns our attention from our *own* work to that of others. When beginning this journey, it's all too easy to be overwhelmed by all the minimalist inspiration and information and the sheer number of people who appear to have it figured out. Add in a family or significant other who is resistant to the idea of owning less, and comparison can pull you under. As messy minimalists, we avoid the trappings of comparison and accept early on that our children's hoarding of rocks and action figures doesn't move minimalism out of reach for us. A picture-perfect playroom is not the goal here. Thank goodness.

We are in this to clear the clutter and unearth the things that matter most to us so that we can wholeheartedly pursue an undistracted life of purpose.

We are in this to clear the clutter and unearth the things that matter most to us so that we can wholeheartedly pursue an undistracted life of purpose. Let the images and stories of other minimalists become inspiration rather than a source of discouragement. Flip the narrative. If you find you're comparing yourself to others, put that comparison to work for you and instead, let it turn into *hope*. If they can do it, so can you! If *I* can do it, so can you. Don't compare where you are right now with where someone else is when they've been at it for years. This is *your* story. Let their minimalist story motivate you to put one foot in front of the other and continue with your own.

2. Settle for Good Enough—for Now

Most of the minimalists I know, myself included, didn't declutter every area of their homes perfectly in one orderly and efficient swoop. We did it in waves. Some larger than others. Think of this initial stage as just the first draft of your minimalism. It's likely going to take a few revisions.

When we started purging our home, I thought we'd for sure have it done in three months tops! It ended up taking us a full year to go through every area of our home. We've gone through it a number of times since. Don't be alarmed if it takes multiple passes before you get to a place where it begins to feel light and fit the life you're crafting. As you add more people to your family, or kids begin to move away, the amount of stuff you need will change as well. Remember: this is real life.

3. Start Simple, but Not Too Simple

When choosing which area of your home to declutter first, don't bite off more than you can chew. Your biggest problem area isn't necessarily the best place to begin. Choose an area of your home that will provide the biggest reward with the least amount of resistance. That area will not be the same area for everybody. Simple is relative.

Beginning in my wardrobe felt simple to me. I've never been overly attached to clothing. Decluttering my closet felt like an easy yet significant first step. It wasn't an overly emotional undertaking. Yet once it was cleared of clutter, I felt motivated and empowered to keep going.

Now if I had started in our basement, kitchen, or garage, Paul would have for sure come home that evening to find me eating a bowl of raw cookie dough and telling him, "I've made a huge mistake." I hadn't developed strong enough decluttering muscles yet. I didn't know how to take on a project of that magnitude. I needed more experience first. As you press on, you'll grow more decisive. You'll spend less and less time second-guessing yourself and begin to move through your home at a faster pace. It's muscle memory.

· On the other hand, if you start in *too* insignificant of an area of your home, it will be difficult to gain momentum and really feel the positive effects of less in your everyday life. Think through which area of your home will provide the biggest bang for your buck. Only you can gauge where exactly that is; the odds are good, though, that it's *not* your family photos, attic, or storage unit.

If you need a little more help deciding where to begin, below is a helpful four-step exercise for choosing exactly that. The first step, as you'll see, is to figure out the three most cluttered spaces in your home (excluding the areas that aren't yours to declutter, such as your kids' toys or your spouse's workshop or craft closet). I'm talking about the areas so cluttered you've wondered if you'd be better off if they just caught fire so you could start fresh. (You know, assuming the fire was well contained and nobody was home. I mean, let's not be total lunatics about this.)

1. What are the three most cluttered areas in your home?

MINE

Basement storage area

Kitchen

Garage

YOURS

_____

_____

_____

2. What are the five most used areas of your home?

MINE

Coat closet

Kitchen

Bathroom

My closet

Garage

YOURS

_____

_____

_____

_____

_____

3. Now cross off any areas that made it into both lists. I do not recommend beginning to declutter your home in any area that is also one of your most stress-inducing areas.

MINE	YOURS
Coat closet	_____
~~Kitchen~~	_____
Bathroom	_____
My closet	_____
~~Garage~~	_____

4. Now you must choose where you'll begin. For example, the three areas left on my list were our coat closet, bathroom, and my closet. I want you to choose an area of your home that would provide the biggest impact on your day-to-day life. For me, that was my clothing, and that's exactly where I began.

THIS REQUIRES MORE CONSISTENCY THAN INTENSITY

I've been coaching my son's soccer team since he was in second grade. I've got to tell you, it's been a wild ride from the very beginning. During any given soccer practice, I find myself going through something similar to the five stages of grief.

Denial: I can't believe I signed up for this job. *Anger*: If one more kid drop-kicks a ball into the woods while I'm explaining how offside works for the millionth time, I'm shutting down this whole team! *Bargaining*: Please. Please. I beg you guys. Let's just do this one last drill and then we'll scrimmage. *Depression*: Fine. Fine. Let's just scrimmage. I don't even care. I'm the worst coach ever. *Acceptance*: Oh wow! Would you look at that footwork? I think they're actually beginning to work together as a team. These kids are improving every week. *I'm amazing.*

In all seriousness, it's the best job ever, and I love these kids dearly, even when I look like I'm about to snap. Which is almost at every practice.

I've had a front-row view for four years now, watching them slowly improve with time. Yet I can't recall any one particular practice or drill that made all the difference. It's the consistency that allows for the improvement. It all adds up, compounds, and snowballs. Consistently showing up, getting as many touches on the soccer ball as possible: that's what made way for improvement—even if they are secretly munching on pockets full of fruit snacks while running laps.

As you grow more comfortable with letting go and more confident in your own resourcefulness, you'll begin to let go at an even faster rate, creating space in areas that once seemed impossible.

The same goes for decluttering your home. For days, weeks, or even months on end, you may feel as though you're actually making it worse. The mess, the piles, and the stress of it all can make you feel like your home is a lost cause. Hang in there, even if only at a snail's pace. The consistency has a snowball effect. Every day builds on the last. As you grow more comfortable with letting go and more confident in your own resourcefulness, you'll begin to let go at an even faster rate, creating space in areas that once seemed impossible.

Keep showing up, even when you want to pull your hair out. Eventually you're going to find your hard work paying off, and you'll think to yourself: *I'm amazing.*

MESSY MINIMALIST TIP: START EVEN SMALLER

If short on time or hesitant to tackle a large area, opt to declutter a smaller subcategory of your home instead. Set a fifteen-minute timer and start writing that first draft of your minimalist story. Instead of tackling the kitchen, just declutter mugs or Tupperware. Go through the coats in your coat closets, the T-shirts in your wardrobe, or the dental floss in your bathroom. Remember every small win is forward progress, reinforcing your identity-based goal and eventually snowballing into bigger accomplishments. It all counts. Just get started.

PART III

DECLUTTERING YOUR SPACE

12

HOW TO BEGIN

You don't have to get it right, you just have to get it going.
—Mike Litman

I started wearing glasses during my junior year of high school. My American history teacher, Ms. Ryckman, pulled me aside after class and suggested I may want to get my eyes checked. Turns out not everybody has to squint their way through class.

My new prescription wasn't all that strong, but it was strong enough that I could finally tell that trees off in the distance had leaves. I just assumed everyone saw them as blurry green blobs. Who knew? I mostly wore my glasses in class, at the movie theater, and when driving at night. The longer I wore them, though, the more I grew to rely on them to clearly see farther than fifteen feet in front of me.

Fast forward almost a decade later: while planning my wedding, I realized it would be nice to clearly see the man I was about to marry as I walked down the aisle without having to wear the glasses I'd been wearing only intermittently. So I made an appointment with my optometrist and got myself some contacts.

In all the excitement during the weeks leading up to that blissful day, it never crossed my mind that it might be a good idea to maybe, just once, practice putting contacts in my eyes. In fact, I completely forgot about them until the moment the wedding photographer said he was ready to start snapping photos.

I panicked, quickly peeled back the lid from my contacts' plastic packaging, fumbled to pick up a contact, and tried to place this tiny little silicone circle onto my eyeball for the very first time in my entire life. As you might imagine, waiting until the moment before your wedding photos is not the best time to start poking yourself in the eye.

I had no idea what I was doing. With every awkward attempt, my eyes grew redder and more watery, threatening to breach the makeup I'd paid good money to have applied. It started to seem as though my only options were to either wear my glasses or marry a blurry penguin man.

Thankfully my bridesmaid Jessica, a longtime friend and wearer of contacts, saw what was happening and took charge. Like a true friend, she grabbed that contact out of my fumbling fingers, directed my gaze to the wall, and confidently stuck her actual finger into my eye. It's this kind of friendship—the grab-you-by-the-shoulders, here-let-me-do-it, shove-you-in-the-right-direction, poke-you-in-the-eyeball kind—that makes this unpredictable life doable.

When I brainstorm with my simplicity-focused friend Becky, or when I chat on social media with like-hearted friends from around the world about the perks and struggles of minimalism, it provides greater clarity than when I go it alone. On top of that, it challenges me to go further, holds me accountable, and gives me permission to let go. Sometimes a nod of approval from a comrade in the thick of it is really all we need. We are meant for community. All of us. And not just when it comes to this messy minimalism thing either. No. Life itself is messy. People get crappy diseases, we lose parents, babies won't latch on, and our opinionated children try to break us, regularly. I can't even begin to count the number of times I've needed a friend to either scoop me up off the floor or smack me across the face and say: "Pull it together, woman!"

I know I can rely on Carolyn to invite me to work out with her when she knows I'm in a slump. I need Stacey to just tell it like it is, Effie to remind me of who I am, and Becky to drop that awkward question: "So how are you doing spiritually?" I need them. Each of them.

> *Between the advertisers attempting to pull you back in and your extended family second-guessing your every attempt at minimalism, it's easy to grow discouraged.*

If you're going to do this—if you're going to swim against the current, ditch the excess, and journey toward a simpler yet more meaningful life—you're going to need a comrade by your side, even if that only looks like this book for now. I got you, friend.

Between the advertisers attempting to pull you back in and your extended family second-guessing your every attempt at minimalism, it's easy to grow discouraged. You'll need trusted people headed in the same direction to remind you who you are and the course you've set for yourself. If finding a minimalist companion or community proves to be slow going, take heart and keep at it. I've found the simple life to be rather contagious. The community may just find you.

As you get uncluttered, choose less on purpose, set your sights on simple, and live a countercultural lifestyle, you'll occasionally lose your way. What you'll need is a community, or even just one single person, whether online or in real life, willing to stick their finger in your eyeball so you can focus more clearly on what's most important.

BEGIN WITH YOU

If you have a family living in your home, odds are good you'll be tempted to begin your minimalist journey by decluttering their stuff first. Their stuff always seems like the bigger problem and the easier items to ditch. Trust me, I know the feeling of wanting to tackle your husband's sock drawer with a lighter in one hand and a cocktail in the other. I've watched my kids pull every toy we own onto the floor, then walk away to play with the remote control or, worse, look me in the eye and dare to tell me they're bored. Jesus, take the wheel.

It is, however, imperative that you ignore the urge to begin trashing their stuff first and do the deep work of starting with your own. It will offer you a chance to gain wisdom, credibility, and empathy when it comes time to help them tackle their belongings.

When I headed home from church on day one, ready to take on the clutter in my home, the first place I started was my very own closet. However, that's not at all where I *wanted* to start. No, I wanted to get rid of the toys. Every last one of them if I could. I pictured burning the excess toys in a massive, ceremonial bonfire, cleansing us of all clutter forever. I truly thought my kids' stuff was the problem. Fortunately, when I arrived home, it was lunchtime, and my kiddos needed to eat. While I waited for the grilled cheese to ~~burn~~ brown, I googled, "How to become a minimalist." What I found changed my mind. I came across an article by Joshua Becker of *Becoming Minimalist* in which he addresses this all-too-common misstep. He suggested this: "Minimize your personal belongings first and your shared family belongings second. It would be unfair to ask your child/teenager to thoroughly adopt the lifestyle until you have done it personally. Also remember, you will learn valuable lessons when you remove your personal clutter—valuable lessons that will put you in a better place to help your son or daughter navigate their journey."

Well, crap. That wasn't the advice I wanted to read at all. While every fiber of my being wanted to head directly to the toy box in my kids' room, I knew he was right. If this was for real—if we were really going to do this thing—I had to go first. That's what parents do anyway. We stick our hands in the bathwater to test the temperature. We taste the macaroni and cheese to make sure it's cooled enough to serve (although let's be honest: taste testing Kraft Mac & Cheese isn't much of a sacrifice, is it?). You get it.

> *When it comes to minimalism and the deep work of getting rid of our excess stuff, we've got to go first. How can we ever help our families navigate their own journeys if we have never traveled this narrow and winding path ourselves?*

When it comes to minimalism and the deep work of getting rid of our excess stuff, we've got to go first. How can we ever help our families navigate their own journeys if we have never traveled this narrow and winding path ourselves? Besides, our kids aren't the ones who got us into this mess in the first place. It was us. We are the ones who steered this ship so far off course. It's up to us to lead it back.

BE TEACHABLE

A few years back, I found myself in my first ever yoga class. A friend of mine was an instructor in training at the time, and I was eager to be both supportive and get my post-baby body moving again. Which, for the record, occurs at a much slower pace after baby number three. Sigh.

The class began innocently enough. We were instructed to let go of the morning and release the tension in our shoulders, jaws, and hearts. I worked *hard* to focus on not focusing, which felt like it may have just been the most difficult part about this entire yoga class. That is until the instructor started to put the word *power* in power yoga. In a matter of minutes, I found myself gasping, my arms shaking, and my face dripping with sweat. I'm not sure, but it's quite possible even my eyeballs were sweating that day. The instructor moved through the flows at a ridiculous tempo for a newbie like me, using names for postures I'd never heard before. I hated it and loved it at the very same time.

I kept my eye on my friend, who has the ability to hop into a handstand with the same ease with which I sip a cup of coffee, to mimic her movements when I got confused. Which was often.

The actual instructor circled through the room, occasionally adjusting people's postures and offering personal instruction. She veered toward me as I struggled to simply keep my arms above my head. (Who would have thought something so simple could require so much effort?) She placed her hands on my shoulders as a gentle reminder to relax them. I did.

This instructor continued to make the rounds for the remainder of the class. Each time she neared me I would tighten and relax, twist and lift, plant and spread, and do all I could to get myself into what felt like the right pose. Every time she passed by without correcting me made me feel like I was totally nailing this yoga thing.

Eventually this ninety-minute ~~torture session~~ yoga class came to an end, and somehow, I found the strength to peel my Jell-O body off the mat. Disoriented and saturated in sweat, I rolled up my mat as my friend asked me how I liked it. I told her it was touch and go there for a while, and I never thought I was going to live through it, but that ultimately, I was hooked. Before this conversation came to an end, I mentioned how proud I felt every time the instructor walked past me without having to correct my posture.

She graciously smiled and responded with, "Oh, I *love* when she corrects me. There is always some way I can improve my posture."

I didn't think much of her comment at the time, probably because I could barely even find my way to the exit. But it came to mind just last week when I found myself standing mat-to-mat with that same dear friend.

This time as that same instructor rounded my mat, I tightened and relaxed, twisted and lifted, planted and spread, just like before. Only this time, two years later, I, too, hoped to be corrected. I wanted her to show me how I could improve. How I could twist a little deeper, sink a little lower, stand a little taller. I reflected on what was different this time, knowing it couldn't possibly be improved flexibility or yoga terminology competency.

It was teachability.

Becoming teachable was new to me—not because I refused to be but because I didn't know I needed to be. I thought the best way to get through life was by remaining confident and consistent in what you know. The trouble with that is this: What we know isn't always the best way, the right way, or the only way. What works for you when you're eighteen won't work when you're twenty-eight and it certainly won't work when you're thirty-eight.

There are many different methods, theories, and hacks when it comes to decluttering your home to live with less. Like I've said before, there is no one right way to do this. One thing I've found to be imperative, though, on this imperfectly perfect minimalist journey is to keep an open and teachable mind. Don't assume anything *has* to stay or *has* to go. Don't assume you've mastered any of it, ever. Rather, be willing to get uncomfortable and rethink the way you do things.

Maybe that one specific bowl you use for that one specific task can actually be used to do the job of many. I recall holding onto one particular dish simply because we used it to microwave one-minute oatmeal. Never mind the fact that I had a million bowls capable of microwaving one-minute oatmeal.

Sure, it was just one bowl; but it's that kind of rigid and inflexible thinking that keeps our cabinets cluttered. Be willing to shake things up, do things a bit differently. Trust me, maintaining the status quo is much more work in the long run. Teachability begins by first acknowledging that we don't have it all figured out, which in my experience, is the hardest part of all. After that you're looking at nothing but new opportunities for growth. Besides, one-minute oatmeal covered in brown sugar tastes the same no matter which bowl you microwave it in.

This whole decluttering-your-life thing involves a lot of trial and error. I promise you'll keep too much at first. But then you might declutter your child's wardrobe so severely that finding clean pants before school is next to impossible. A side note: if you find scraping hummus off your daughter's leggings with your thumbnail at seven o'clock in the morning is becoming a regular occurrence, it might be time to add an extra pair of leggings to her wardrobe. Just speaking from experience.

Getting it wrong plays just as important a role as getting it right. It's all part of the process of curating a home that serves your real life. Remember: just as you can't possibly know how to play "Somewhere over the Rainbow" the first time you pick up your ukulele, neither will you know exactly what needs to stay and what needs to go the moment you begin to clear the excess. It takes lots of mistimed strums, failed attempts at handstands, and hummus-scraping moments to find what works best for you. Don't forget: there's always some way to improve your posture.

MESSY MINIMALIST TIP: JOIN A BOOK CLUB

Did you know that 27 percent of US adults haven't read even part of a book in the last year? It wasn't until just a few years ago that I myself became a reader. In fact, I left college with a degree and an educational hangover, assuming both exempted me from having to learn something new ever again.

As you make space in your home and margin in your calendar—we'll get to that a few chapters from now—I suggest using some of your newfound time and energy to invest in your own personal growth. Read a book on a new topic (the Enneagram is one of my favorites). Consider joining or even creating a book club to get other people's perspectives on what you're reading. It's incredible how two people can read the same book and walk away having learned something totally different. Oh, and if this happens to be the first book you've read this year, I'm honored.

13

HOW TO CREATE A
CLUTTER-FREE HOME

Your home is living space, not storage space.

—Francine Jay

Let's get down to business.

I truly wish I could pop on over with a latte, muffin, and my awkward enthusiasm for decluttering to help you go through every single area of your home. I really do. Maybe someday. For now, we'll have to settle for this book.

My favorite part of having minimized my own possessions has been gaining the knowledge and experience to help others do the same. I weirdly *love* helping people get rid of their stuff. Sometimes it's a simple consultation, as we dream up what could be. But every now and then someone will let me climb on top of their kitchen counters and start gutting cabinets. That's my favorite part.

We've spent a lot of time talking about the *whys* and *whats* of minimalism, and we've addressed vital mindset shifts that must take place in order to maintain our clutter-free lives. It's time now to get our hands dirty and tackle the *how*. I'm going to lay out a four-step process to get you on your way. However, becoming a messy minimalist is never as simple as following a step-by-step process. It won't all work for you. That's okay. Just pocket the tips you find helpful and leave the rest behind.

1. DECIDE ON YOUR DONATION DROP-OFF LOCATIONS BEFORE YOU DECLUTTER

The very first thing I want you to do is to decide, ahead of time, where you're going to take your donation items. This is important for two reasons.

First, if you don't have a place to take your donation items, they will likely end up sitting in a corner of your home or the trunk of your car for far too long. The longer you look at them, the more likely it is you'll start to second-guess your decision to donate certain items and start pulling them out of those bags and boxes. Second, when you intentionally choose a specific donation location that aligns with your heart, letting go becomes a whole lot easier.

> *When you know your excess stuff is being put to good use and actually filling real needs in your community, it's so much easier to let go.*

For my preferred donation drop spots, I decided to donate my daughter's clothes to a family friend with twin girls, all baby items to our pregnancy service center, and most everything else to our local city rescue mission thrift store. There, the sale of my donated items supports our city's local rescue mission, which feeds, houses, and provides hope to hundreds of individuals in my hometown every day.

It's more difficult to justify keeping extra stuff I don't really need when I've got an address for a person or place that could use it. When you know your excess stuff is being put to good use and actually filling real needs in your community, it's so much easier to let go.

Another factor to consider when deciding where to drop your items off is logistics. Do you have a donation site nearby? Choosing a site in close proximity can make donation drop-off as convenient as getting a latte on your way to work.

2. DIVIDE THE CONTENTS OF YOUR SPACE INTO FOUR CATEGORIES

Now that you've decided on both the space you'll declutter first (see chapter 11) and your drop-off location, go ahead and begin to empty that space. Brace yourself: it's going to get worse before it gets better. But stick with me, and it *will* get better.

If you've chosen your bathroom, empty every drawer and shelf. If it's your closet, begin pulling shirts off the hangers one by one. Touch, inspect, and even smell each and every item if necessary. Contemplate how and when you use it.

Don't forget to gather the items throughout your home that are *supposed* to be in this space but have gotten moved around. For example, if you're working through your linen closet, don't forget about the towels hanging over the shower curtain, or if you're working on your medicine cabinet, remember the medications that have migrated into a kitchen cabinet. If you're tackling your wardrobe, you'll want to be sure and include the off-season attire stored in the basement or beneath your bed.

Do not, however, make completing all the laundry a prerequisite for beginning this project. That is a classic perfectionist move. You, friend, are a messy minimalist, and we don't wait until everything is in order to declutter our lives. We simply take the time we have to accomplish what we can.

As you remove items from your space, divide them into four categories: donate, trash, sell, or keep.

Donate

Note that I said four *categories*, not four *piles*. Your donation category may slowly morph into what looks like thirty smaller piles. You may find shirts your sister could use for work; unused bath products to donate to a women's shelter; baby items you can drop off at your local pregnancy services center; and books you can donate to your children's school library. For those larger items that aren't so easy to haul away, you can pop them up on a local Freecycle group or simply list them as *free* on Facebook Marketplace or Craigslist.

> *If you're frustrated by the quantity of items you're sending to the landfill, know this: trashing it now is not the mistake; buying it in the first place was.*

I've read advice from other minimalists warning against this kind of behavior. They suggest that trying to coordinate dropping off your things to multiple organizations and people only adds unnecessary work to an already difficult process. They are right: it is absolutely more work this way. More driving. More communicating. More orchestrating. Personally, though, I think customizing your donations is a great thing. This way you're giving your excess stuff the best chance to get used by the people who need it.

Now that said, if you do decide to simply drop it all off at the nearest Goodwill, I won't blame you one bit. Just keep in mind that you may be able to let go of even *more* stuff when you know it's going to serve a purpose you're passionate about.

Trash

While I do suggest donating and recycling as much as possible, the sad reality is that you probably own plenty of stuff nobody wants. That can be really tough to accept. Even when we know that be true, trashing unneeded items still tends to leave us feeling guilty and wasteful, which in turn causes us to keep items we shouldn't.

If you're frustrated by the quantity of items you're sending to the landfill, know this: trashing it now is not the mistake; buying it in the first place was. You already paid for it. Whether you, your children, or your children's children trash it, it will one day end up in a landfill. There's just no way around it. Letting it clutter up your home for the rest of your life won't change that fact. To live uncluttered, you must let go of it. Instead of holding on, let that remorse be a catalyst for changing the way you purchase and accumulate for the rest of your days on this earth.

Sell

I believe we need to hold this category loosely. Yes, selling your excess possessions can go a long way toward paying off debt, funding a weekend trip, or providing added motivation to rid your home of its too muchness. But those good intentions can result in you holding on for far too long. Letting go of an item should never become contingent on the sale of that item.

Go ahead and list that item on Facebook Marketplace, Craigslist, or eBay, or set a date for your garage sale, preferably for as soon as humanly possible. Do your best to sell the items you believe hold value within a predetermined amount of time for a very, *very* reasonable amount of money. If you want it gone fast—and you do—you need to price it in such a way that it will sell. If somebody buys it, great! If not, donate it. End of story.

A good rule of thumb is to list an item for about 30 percent of what it costs new, assuming it's in excellent condition. Nobody is going to pay top dollar for your broken lamp. Keep it listed for three to five days. If you don't get any takers, pull down the listing and donate it.

Don't let yourself get caught up in thinking "But I spent this much on it" or "This is worth so much more!" It's so easy to fall prey to the clutter trap of overvaluing our junk. Our stuff is only worth what someone will pay for it. Don't hold on indefinitely, hoping to find someone who values it as highly as you do.

Keep

This is when I most wish I could pop out of this book like a Star Wars Jedi hologram to talk you through the specific items you own, offering advice on which to keep and which to ditch. *Patience you must have, my young Padawan.* Ultimately, you're going to have to make these decisions yourself, and it will require that you give yourself lots of grace in the process. You can do this; I know you can.

> *It's so easy to fall prey to the clutter trap of overvaluing our junk. Our stuff is only worth what someone will pay for it.*

There is no formulaic list of questions I can offer, no perfect equation or exact science for figuring out what to own. It comes down to you: trusting yourself to make the call, admitting you won't get it right every time, knowing your new minimalist mindset has equipped you with the skills you need to live and own with greater intention. Trust your resourcefulness, embrace faith in God's provision, and acknowledge the benefits of white space. You, my messy minimalist friend, only keep the items that add to your meaningful life. You let go of the ones that get in the way.

Here are a handful of questions to bring clarity to this decision.

- Would I buy this item again?
- Does this item add any value to my life?
- Would I miss this item if it were gone for good?
- Is this a duplicate?
- Do I have something else that can perform the same task as this item?
- Do I like looking at this item?
- Is this item worth taking care of?
- Do I really need this item?
- Do I love this item?
- Can I get by just fine without it?

- Would someone else get more use out of this item than me?
- Am I only keeping this item because it's trending right now?

Consider these questions a jumping-off point. If you really wanted to, you could find a justification for keeping just about every single item in your home. Now is the time to lean on your new minimalist mindset and dare to do differently.

Once your space is fully emptied and your possessions divided into four categories—keep, donate, sell, and trash—go ahead and begin to put that "keep" pile away. As you do so, reassess what you've decided to keep. Have you selected far too many "favorite mugs?" Did you keep twelve sweaters but realize now that's likely more than you'll ever wear? Is your undergarment drawer still overflowing? Putting everything away offers us another opportunity to cull a little more deeply.

Take time to enjoy the progress you've made, no matter how small.

It's very easy to get sidetracked during the decluttering process—especially if you happen upon lost items or uncover a project you gave up on long ago. One minute you're decluttering a shelf in your linen closet and the next thing you know you're chalk painting a picture frame or searching eBay for a replacement button. Stay on task!

3. GET RID OF YOUR PILES ASAP

I don't mean to be the boss of you, but get that stuff you've decided to let go of out of your house as soon as possible! When we let our donation items linger in our homes, we leave too many opportunities to second-guess ourselves. If you have small children in your home, it's even more important. No matter how well you think you've hidden that pile of toys ready for donation, they'll find it. They always do. And when they do, it won't take long for those toys to once again be redistributed throughout your home. Side note: I highly recommend using black trash bags or closeable cardboard boxes to donate your kids' items. Even if they agreed to letting go of those excess toys, watching you waltz into the thrift store carrying their stuff will be difficult. Using a dark trash bag or cardboard box makes that discomfort easily avoidable.

4. TREAT YOURSELF (BUT NOT WITH MORE STUFF)

Once you've completed decluttering a space, it's time to treat yourself. Just don't treat yourself to more stuff.

Burnout plays a major role in causing people to give up. Take time to enjoy the progress you've made, no matter how small. Read a book in your newly decluttered bedroom, celebrate with a family game night now that cleanup takes less time, or splurge on a nice dinner out with all that money you've saved. Find small ways to consistently revel in your progress. You've earned it, friend!

MESSY MINIMALIST TIP: DECLUTTER ONE BOX AT A TIME

If you're in need of a slower approach to decluttering, place a box in every major room of your home. As you go about your day and come across items you no longer need, place them in the box. Once the box is filled, donate it. Note: I do not recommend this method if you have little ones at home. They'll likely just empty your boxes over and over again.

14

HOW TO DECLUTTER YOUR KITCHEN, LIVING ROOM, AND CLOSETS

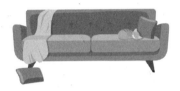

Just because we have the space, doesn't mean we should fill it.
—Zoë Kim

It's time to get specific. Well, as specific as I can be without a house call. In this chapter, you won't find a one-size-fits-all shopping list of gadgets you should add to your minimalist kitchen or a list of stuff you're no longer allowed to own. You know by now I don't roll that way.

I bake pies; you may not. Maybe you air fry your vegetables, but I don't. Instead of following a framework, I want to simply invite you to reassess what you keep and why. From your kitchen to your closet, ask yourself this: Which items do I just *assume* I need and which do I *actually* need?

The benefits of a clutter-free life outweigh the benefits of let's say, keeping a garlic press if you only ever use pre-minced garlic from a jar. Could one cheese grater be sufficient? If so, why do you own three? Be honest. Be ruthless. Be generous. And most importantly, be open to changing the way you do things.

THE CLUTTERED KITCHEN THEORY

We've heard it said: the kitchen is the heart of the home. It's true. The kitchen is the hub for all things in and out. It's where life happens. It's where we make meals, discuss pressing issues, help kids with homework, and huddle around a bowl of raw cookie dough, willingly throwing salmonella caution to the wind in exchange for a heaping spoonful of goodness. Here we drop our mail, schoolwork, used travel mugs, and half-finished art projects. Tiny or large, updated or outdated, it doesn't matter: the kitchen is the most used and most seen room in every home.

I've got a theory about the power a kitchen exerts in a living space that I've seen confirmed over and over again. Which is why, while you shouldn't necessarily take on decluttering your kitchen first, when you do, it will likely have the single greatest positive impact on your home.

Just as clutter begets clutter, so does minimalism beget minimalism.

My cluttered kitchen theory says this: A cluttered kitchen invites clutter into every other room of your home. Because of this, when the kitchen is in disarray, the rest of the home lends itself more freely to mess and clutter. On the flip side, when the kitchen is tidy, orderly, and simplified, we feel more inclined to maintain the rest of the home at that same level. The kitchen either raises or lowers the bar, setting the tone for the entire home.

When you see what a clutter-free kitchen can do for your peace of mind, you'll want it in every room of your home, and you'll fight to maintain it. Just as clutter begets clutter, so does minimalism beget minimalism. The kitchen is my favorite room to help others declutter because it has a wide-reaching impact throughout the rest of the home.

CONVENIENCE FALLACY

One of the reasons we often allow clutter to rule in the kitchen is the convenience fallacy. I first read about this concept in the book *The Minimalist Home* by Joshua Becker. This is how he describes it: "There are certain places in our homes where we tend to leave items out because we think it will make it easier for us to grab them. . . . By leaving these things out, we think we're saving time when we need them. We think we are simplifying our lives." Becker later describes how the convenience fallacy affects the kitchen: "These items spend far more time as clutter than they do as needed instruments of food preparation. For example, if you make toast for breakfast, it will take you roughly three minutes to toast your bread. After that, the toaster will sit unused for the next twenty-three hours and fifty-seven minutes."

Nowhere is the convenience fallacy more evident than in the kitchen. On our countertops, we house items such as vitamins, stand mixers, diffusers, blenders, toasters, spice racks, paper towels, knives, breads, and that waffle maker we only use on Saturdays. All day, every day, all in the name of simplicity and convenience, we allow clutter to rule.

Keeping appliances, spatulas, and cutting boards within arm's reach may seem like the easiest option, but it's not. It's just what you're used to. In fact, when you first clear off your counters, it may even look really weird to you. Almost uncomfortably weird. But I've found it only takes a day or so for your eyes and your mind to adjust to the sight of empty space. Once you see it—I mean *deeply* see the calm that empty spaces can provide—you can't unsee it.

DECLUTTERING YOUR KITCHEN

Every good ole fashion kitchen declutter begins with leggings, a pot of coffee, a "before" photo—obviously—and some good music. That is if you aren't simultaneously trying to distract littles ones. If that's the case for you, my friend, then you're likely listening to the sound of PBS KIDS or Disney+ streaming in the background.

So how exactly do you clear those counters that are currently peppered with appliances, spices, and vitamins? In order to achieve clear counter status, you must first make space in those overstuffed cabinets of yours. Start by emptying them one by one, sorting your items into the keep, donate, sell, and trash categories that we talked about in chapter 13.

If you're feeling overwhelmed or having trouble deciding which treacherous cabinet to open first, start by sifting through your food storage containers. Ditch the random lids and lidless containers. Boom! From there move to your mixing bowls, then on to the spatulas and gadgets. Keep your head down, nose to the grindstone, and music pumping until you've officially made a total disaster of your kitchen. Remember: it gets worse before it gets better. Move through your cabinets like a rebel without a cause. Except you have a cause—a worthy one. You're making space for sanity, room for what matters most, and a spot for that blender, one cluttered cabinet at a time.

Consolidate

It didn't take long for me to realize just how many items I had that were capable of performing the exact same task. Do we really need multiple whisks of varying sizes? Can a good knife do the job of an apple slicer, cheese slicer, pizza slicer, and avocado slicer? The answer is yes (well, I found the pizza slicer to be essential, but maybe that isn't the case for you). Would you even notice if a few mixing bowls went to the thrift store so your lazy Susan could accommodate your blender and mixer? Look for the items you can use to perform multiple tasks.

Box It Up

Decluttering can be nerve-racking, especially if you have a tendency to succumb to the what-ifs. If you find yourself hesitating to let go of something even when you know you don't need it, try boxing it up and sitting on it for a few weeks. Stash it in the garage or basement, giving yourself time to both experiment with and experience the benefits of a clutter-free kitchen. The courage to let go will follow.

My Favorite Kitchen Items

Your kitchen, from its paint color to the items within it, is unique to you. That's how it should be. I was tempted to add a list of nonessential kitchen items to this chapter—things you should let go of as a jumping-off point. You know, a list of "Twenty-Five Kitchen Items to Declutter Today." But I deleted it because the essentials are not universal.

Instead, I decided to list a few of *my* favorite kitchen essentials. These are items that I have no intention of decluttering. Keep in mind, this list likely includes items you'd consider to be the very definition of clutter. But that's the point, right? To create a home that serves you and your uniqueness. So get to it.

- A small collection of eclectic, vintage coffee mugs
- Electric pressure cooker
- Pastry-dough cutter
- Block set of knives
- Air popper popcorn maker
- *Two* rolling pins
- Cake stand and frosting gun
- Fat separator
- Wine opener
- Kitchen scissors
- Coffee maker
- Stand mixer

Does everybody need a pastry-dough cutter or a sixty-year-old coffee mug in their kitchen? Nope. While we eliminated our fondue pot, electric wok, and pasta maker, those may be things you use on a regular basis. It's time to create the space for the things your individual kitchen requires by confidently letting go of what it doesn't.

FROM LINEN CLOSETS TO FAMILY ROOMS

My home doesn't boast an excessive number of large closets. We currently live in a three-bedroom, two-story, 1,890-square-foot home with a two-car garage and a partially finished basement. We partially finished our basement prior to minimalism, in an effort to "contain our kids' toys" (spits coffee out laughing). Turns out, kids don't like their things contained anywhere. It simply became a dumping ground for the toys they never played with—and the Bermuda Triangle for everything they did. It's a decent-sized home, that's for sure, but nothing the average-sized US family couldn't clutter up in a matter of minutes.

As I look back on that first year of decluttering, one thing that sticks out to me is the number of times the purpose of a specific space changed. As we cleared the nooks and crannies, we repurposed the way they served our family time and time again. For example, our then-linen closet is now a game closet. While once overflowing with extra sheets, towels, and the most random items, it's now home to our board games, craft supplies, and gift bags. (Yes, I keep a small stash of used gift bags. I *hate* buying new gift bags.)

We used to store our board games in the corner of our living room, between a bookshelf and couch ... on the floor. Our system was one part convenience fallacy and three parts nowhere else to put them. It stresses me out to even think about it now. While we knew it wasn't the *best* solution, we saw no other option. We figured it was our home's fault. If *only* our floor plan featured a first-floor game closet, *then* those games would have a home. Clearly it was the architect's fault that we were living such a cluttered existence. As we decluttered our entire home, those games moved off the floor to the bookshelf, then into our coat closet, before finally landing in a more permanent home.

The point I'm trying to make here is this: keep going and be flexible. You may not find the best solution for your stuff on day one. The more excess stuff you clear from your home, the more space you'll create. Keep that open and teachable mindset and be willing to slowly experiment with how you use your space. Nothing has to be permanent. Don't let the fact that it isn't perfect on the first day halt your efforts and send you phoning a realtor in search of a bigger and better home. Dig in, keep clearing space after space, and eventually you'll find a solution to that problem area.

This is exactly why now is not the time to invest in an organizational or storage system. As the clutter leaves your home, you'll find you have plenty of space to store the stuff you actually use. You just first need to get rid of the stuff you don't.

MESSY MINIMALIST TIP:
KITCHEN ACCESSORIES CAN MULTITASK

Look for kitchen accessories that can play multiple roles in your kitchen. Did you know that a metal ice-cream scooper can also double as a nutcracker and a meat tenderizer? A knife is perfectly capable of mincing garlic, slicing apples, and cutting the foil on a wine bottle. You don't necessarily need a specific gadget for every task.

15

HOW TO DECLUTTER HOME DECOR AND SENTIMENTAL ITEMS

Yes, you can have nice things. Just not white sofas, never buy the white sofas.

—Denaye Barahona

When it comes to home decorating, there are two kinds of people: those who have a knack for it and those who don't. Guess which category I fall into.

Decorating has never been my thing. Even if I somehow managed to come up with a vision in my head for how I wanted a space to look, it would always end up looking wonky, awkward, uneven, and just off. My decorating strategy has always looked like this: See blank space on the wall. Assume something should go there. Head to Hobby Lobby. Find random piece of artwork. Nail to wall, likely crooked.

There: you just passed Cluttered Life Home Decor 101. Congratulations.

I vividly remember the day I decorated our dining and living rooms. We were just days away from having our first child, and due in part to a little thing called "nesting," finding something to hang on those walls became my number-one priority. God forbid I bring my firstborn home from the hospital to a home with bare walls (*eye roll*).

> *What is it that has me feeling like I need something*
> *new, something better, something right now?*

I dragged a friend along with me for this emergency shopping session. Together we ran around the store with just twenty minutes until closing, choosing from whatever was 40 percent off that week. I walked out of the store that evening with an oversized mirror, two shelves, and an extra-large picture of wine bottles. Don't ask me why. We drove it all back to my place, and our husbands spent the remainder of the evening nailing these items to the walls.

There were a few key factors at play that day, the obvious being that I was freaked out about becoming a mom. Instead of addressing what was really going on, I fell victim to the common driving force of consumerism: using retail therapy to cope with the stress. If you tend to use shopping as a means to cope with stress, I want you to know this. You will never fully defeat this beast. It's a battle you'll have to wage time and time again. Even now, after many years of living with less and purchasing with intention, I sometimes feel the urge to run around Target like I'm a contestant on the '90s game show *Supermarket Sweep*.

Now, though, instead of binge shopping and impulsively redecorating, I pause and ask myself why. What is it that has me feeling like I need something new, something better, something right now?

DECORATING THE MESSY MINIMALIST WAY

Maybe it's because you feel overwhelmed by a problem you can't control, or a friend just renovated her kitchen and now yours suddenly feels outdated. Perhaps someone you follow on Instagram posted pictures of their living room, and now you're second-guessing your own wall art. Before you redecorate, it's vital to evaluate *why* you want to do so. Because I can promise you this: within six months of retiling your kitchen backsplash, something newer, trendier, and better is going to make its way to the market. If you haven't wrestled with the deeper issues at play, the cycle of discontentment is going to start all over again.

There is a better way. There is a way to decorate with intention. To love what you own for longer than a single season. Here are three important concepts to keep in mind when decorating as a messy minimalist.

> *Don't assume your home* needs *something. A house or a condo or an apartment is a thing; it doesn't have needs.*

First, don't assume your home *needs* something. A house or a condo or an apartment is a thing; it doesn't have needs. Most of my random decorating purchases occurred after asking questions like, "Does this wall look bare?" or "Does this corner of the room need to be rounded out with an accent piece?"

Your home doesn't *need* a thing. It's quite capable of performing its job without another piece of wall art. It's not sitting there wondering why you don't decorate for Easter, wishing you'd buy newer throw pillows, or silently asking itself why you've left that fireplace mantel so off-balance. This is your home. You should be asking yourself what you *need* from *it*. If you never hang a single piece of artwork, your home will be just fine. In fact, you may find white space and breathing room to be the very things you're looking for.

Next: you do not need to fill all the spaces. One thing I hear over and over when helping people declutter is, "Okay, but what should I put there now?" It's as if once a space is free of clutter, we've got to find something else to fill it with. That is not the case.

Empty space may require an adjustment period. If your empty space looks a little odd at first, I want to challenge you to resist that urge to find something else to place there. Live with it for a few days, and I can almost guarantee you're going to start to love the look of less. Clear space ushers in possibility and creativity, and it accentuates the things that surround it.

I never liked the items I chose that evening. But as a result of decorating my home on an impulse, I spent the next ten years looking at them. We only just recently took them down, donated them, and painted over the many nail holes. Not in exchange for new stuff, but in exchange for white space. Come to find out, that's more my style anyway. Give it a try. It just may be yours as well.

The only thing always trending in the land of less is contentment. Practice that first, and you'll find your home never goes out of style.

Finally: whatever your style is, own it and embrace it. My kitchen is blue. Blue! Do you know how many #minimalistkitchen photos you'll find on Instagram with blue kitchens? As of right now, none. It's a sea of white. Messy minimalists, however, paint their kitchens whatever color they'd like. They ignore what's trendy and let their own style shine. To live with less doesn't require a specific style or look. There isn't a maximum number of framed pictures you're allowed to hang. You don't need to transfer all your spices into mason jars or paint every wall in your home white. The only thing always trending in the land of less is contentment. Practice that first, and you'll find your home never goes out of style.

I was always adding items to my home, hoping one more piece might bring it all together. It wasn't until I stopped accumulating and instead started pulling things off the walls that I was able to see what seems so obvious now. It was breathing room I was searching for all along. My walls didn't need to be balanced out; they needed to be emptied.

Don't be afraid to underdecorate. If you're used to covering every wall and corner of your home with some kind of decor, give white space a chance to prove itself to you. Once your eyes and mindset have had time to adjust, begin to add decor back to your home with greater intention, keeping white space the focal point.

My home isn't what you'd call "up to date." It certainly has more scratches and dings than it does style. But yet, it's here where I thrive. *Less* is what has made my home feel homier than ever before. I never felt more at home in my own home than when I finally stopped trying to make mine look like yours. Instead, I created a space that served me.

SENTIMENTAL ITEMS

I was grossly underprepared for just how emotional I would become when it finally came time to repaint our nursery. It had at one time been the bedroom for each of my babies after they were born. When our youngest and final child aged out of her crib, we moved her into a room with her big sister and rebranded the nursery for our newly nine-year-old boy. He'd shared a room with his sister long enough, and it was time to make the big room swap.

With two years of minimalism under my belt at the time, you'd think a transition like this would be a piece of cake. No such luck. Having that room painted? It wrecked me. Who would have thought a gallon of Urbane Bronze Sherwin Williams paint would elicit such an emotional response?

You see, just before our first child was born, I had a local artist paint a mural on our nursery wall of a tree with a monkey swinging from it. He was a sweet little guy who spent nine years living just above the rocking chair where I nursed my babies, prayed over them, read them stories, and snuggled them after bad dreams.

But my babies weren't babies anymore. The boy I could once throw over my shoulder like a sack of potatoes was becoming a young man who could now lift me. Our potato-swinging days were over. The time had come to replace our little monkey friend with the antlers from my son's first buck.

Here's the thing I've learned through the uncomfortable process of saying goodbye to that monkey: holding on doesn't make their growing up any easier. It won't slow down time or let us relive favorite moments. It simply keeps our arms too full to wholeheartedly embrace the season we're entering.

> *Rather than fixating on what it is you're getting rid of, turn your attention to what you're gaining in return.*

Rather than fixating on what it is you're getting rid of, turn your attention to what you're gaining in return. What will tomorrow look like once you let go? My son is able to brush his own teeth, style his own hair, and do his own laundry. He has even started giving me book recommendations. While he no longer makes us laugh with his adorable preschool cuteness, he has picked up his father's quick wit and has been known to drop some stellar one-liners.

When we remain preoccupied with the past, we miss the amazingness of what is happening before our very eyes. If we hold on to our stuff as if it's a part of who we are, we miss out on the chance to give it a second life. When it came time to let go of our baby gear, I found it much easier to donate the items than to try to sell them. It's hard to put a price tag on items that played such an important role in helping me raise my babies. Knowing they were going to help another parent not only gave me the freedom to let go but also made giving away baby gear feel like the next right step instead of a burden. It wasn't a painful goodbye but a passing of the baton. It was just one mother doing another a favor so she could have her turn soaking up moments with her babies.

A part of me still misses that monkey, but I know he's not really gone. He was just the first layer of paint in the picture of my motherhood.

Heirlooms

Letting go of sentimental items is a complicated undertaking. We often attach memories, relationships, and even love to the items themselves. Doing this can make a difficult task next to impossible. Instead of first deciding what needs to go, I suggest you start by deciding which heirlooms should be put to use.

I drink coffee from my grandmother's mug when I write. She, too, was a writer, and I find her coffee mug to be excellent company, especially on the days I feel stuck. Besides, I'm convinced coffee tastes better from her mug. Go ahead and serve dinner on your grandmother's china, display your dad's beloved book collection, or use one of your aunt's canning jars as a vase to hold wild flowers.

We often hold on to sentimental items as if they are bombs that will detonate if used. We put them in boxes in the basement or the attic for safekeeping. Most of my sentimental items came from my grandmothers. If they ever offered me something of theirs, I gladly said yes, brought it home, wrapped it up, and tucked it away safe and sound, never to be seen or used again. I treasured their hand-me-down items deeply, but that's not how treasured items deserve to be treated. If it's truly a treasure, why not display it, use it, let the light of day shine on it? Yes, it's at greater risk for getting broken when you use it. But at least it will have become a part of your story, just as it was a part of theirs.

Remember: if everything is a treasure, then nothing is really a treasure. It can't all be the same kind of special. Choose the items with the most significance to you and let go of the rest. You are not obligated to keep something just because someone you love once loved it.

When donating heirlooms, it's a good rule of thumb to never donate an item without first checking with family to see if they would like the item. Perhaps that heirloom would get more use or love in the hands of a different member of your family.

Letting go of inherited items can be very difficult. I have come to learn that the fewer items I keep, the more special the ones I own become.

ART PROJECTS AND SCHOOL PAPERS

My youngest child was born just three days before my oldest started kindergarten. It didn't take but a few days before the papers started to roll in. He'd come home from school every day with a backpack loaded with projects and artwork, while I was in absolutely no condition to cull through it all. I was exhausted and practically running on no sleep. With the new baby getting most of my attention, I already felt guilty enough. I wasn't about to start trashing his precious kindergarten projects as well.

Instead, I had my husband pile all of it in the corner of our basement office until I found the time and emotional energy to go through it all. A few months went by before he brought it to my attention again and suggested it was time to address what had now become a bit of a fire hazard.

> *Remember: if everything is a treasure, then nothing is really a treasure. It can't all be the same kind of special.*

I was still a year or so away from becoming a minimalist. But even then, sifting through a mountain of construction paper matted with dried glue stick, I knew keeping even half of it wasn't an option. There were so many papers, and he was only five years old. I started doing the math. At this rate, we'd need a storage unit before he even made it to high school. I was going to need to let go of most of it.

When deciding which school and art projects to keep and which to return to the ground, ask yourself these three questions:

First, did your child actually *make* it? No, I'm not accusing your child of paying a classmate to do their work for them. But if my kid simply took pieces of precut construction paper and glued them to another piece of precut construction paper, I'm not interested in saving it. Those types of projects don't reflect kids' unique imaginations. They were simply following directions. I'm only in the business of saving things that reflect my child's creativity. Things like self-portraits, drawings of our entire family, or that illustration by my third grader of a wagon full of things she'd take with her during a move if she could only take what could fit in a wagon. Those are the things I'll keep.

Next, which one is your favorite? If your child spent the afternoon painting thirty sunsets, decide together on a favorite and let go of the rest.

Last, would you want this from your own childhood? Ask yourself, "If this was *my* kindergarten work and my mother had kept it for me all these years, would I even want it now? What would I do with it today?" I try to imagine which pieces I'd enjoy having from my own childhood—which, for the record, aren't many.

Even after asking those three questions, it's likely that you'll still be looking at a pile of too much stuff. This is when we must create and enforce boundaries. I've designated one medium bin per child to store paperwork and memorabilia. At the beginning and end of every school year, we sift through it and let go of the things that no longer seem as important as they once did in order to make room for new projects.

When it comes to decluttering sentimental items, I've found the physical act of letting go is the hardest part. Once you unclench your fists, open your palms, let go, then turn around, you'll see a clearer path and walk a little lighter into the next season—one full of hope, with new moments yet to be savored. Letting go isn't a bitter ending but a sweet next step. That's true both for you and your stuff.

MESSY MINIMALIST TIP: REVISIT SENTIMENTALS LATER

It's completely normal to find yourself overwhelmed or even stuck, hemming and hawing between letting go or holding on to sentimental items. You're bound to come across items you want to let go of but just can't. If the letting go part just feels too difficult, set it aside and move on to the next thing. Leave it for now and revisit that item a little later in your journey. Remember: grace-based messy minimalists know there's always another opportunity to let go around the corner. Perhaps you need a bit more time to develop those decluttering muscles, or maybe time will tell you that this is an item worth holding on to. Never let the pressure to let go of sentimental items keep you from decluttering the more practical areas in your home.

16

HOW TO CREATE A
MINIMALIST WARDROBE

*You will never find something to wear that makes you feel
beautiful, smart or loved until you believe you already are.*
—Courtney Carver

"Awww, you made it look frumpy."

My longtime friend Stacey has always been my go-to friend for advice
on all things fashion. Girls like me need friends like her. Wildly devoted,
tell-you-exactly-like-it-is kind of friends. Kind and caring, but without
all the candy coating. What would be offensive coming from someone
else feels like valuable information when Stacey says it. Years ago, when
she saw a photo of me in an outfit she had styled for me, her exact words
were, "Awww, you made it look frumpy." What are friends for if not for

total and occasionally even brutal honesty? Odds are good you've got a Stacey in your life too.

They're that friend you vehemently trust with questions like, "Does this match?" "Which boots do you like more?" "Are these sleeves too puffy?" And now: "Did I make this look frumpy?"

I find it important to pause here, just for a second, in order to acknowledge the irony that *I* am now writing a chapter on clothing. I am always the one *getting* fashion advice, never *giving* it. If we've ever crossed paths at school pickup, then you know just how true this is. I'm all about my ripped jeans, flannel button up, and messy bun. For the most part, I consider clothing to be utilitarian. It's for getting around. If I had to label my style, I'd call it Midwest comfy chic. You know, not awful, but definitely comfortable. While I don't aim for frumpy, it's often a by-product of my not really caring all that much.

MINIMALIST STYLE

All that to say: I'm not your Stacey. I won't be telling you which items are frumpy, exactly what to buy, how many pieces to own, or even exactly what to get rid of. In this chapter, you won't find a list of items trending in "minimalist fashion" either. Mostly because I have no clue what's trending right now. Besides, following every new trend is what got us into this mess in the first place, isn't it? We've spent a lifetime accumulating the *latest* things when we should have been focusing our attention and resources on our *favorite* things.

Contrary to what Pinterest may tell you, a minimalist wardrobe doesn't have a specific look. It isn't solely made up of black slacks, white blouses, and tan trench coats. The only thing specific to a minimalist wardrobe is that you've minimized it. Whether you end up with one hundred, thirty-three, or just seven articles of clothing, it doesn't really matter. The point of creating a minimalist wardrobe is to stop letting your clothing keep you from living your life.

If you feel like managing the clothing in your household has become a full-time job in and of itself, it's time to let messy minimalism lighten your load by creating a minimalist capsule wardrobe.

WHAT EXACTLY IS A CAPSULE WARDROBE?

The term *capsule wardrobe* was coined in the 1970s by Susie Faux, a London boutique owner. She defined a capsule wardrobe as containing a few essential and timeless items, such as skirts and pants, that can be supplemented with seasonal pieces. Basically, a capsule wardrobe is a set of clothing in which every article can be mixed and matched and worn together, enabling you to create many outfit combinations from just a few articles of clothing.

I first read about the concept of a capsule wardrobe when I stumbled on the minimalist fashion challenge called Project 333. This is a movement of people committed to wearing just thirty-three items of clothing during any given three-month season—on purpose. It was started by Courtney Carver, who is the author of *Project 333*. Courtney has since become a friend, which makes what I'm about to say just a tad bit awkward.

> *We've spent a lifetime accumulating the* latest *things when we should have been focusing our attention and resources on our* favorite *things.*

I thought Project 333 was insane. Impossible, even. Who in the world would willingly limit themselves to wearing just thirty-three articles of clothing? I rolled my eyes at the very thought of it, assuming it was just another legalistic method to living with less—you know, the perfectionistic, numbers-obsessed form of minimalism I had been so diligently avoiding.

All I could picture were pastel blouses, blazers with shoulder pads, and uncomfortable black dress slacks. That kind of wardrobe is for politicians, not real people. I knew it would never work for my cozy-chic real life. I figured it was simply perfectionism disguised as a tan trench coat, knowing it wouldn't take me long to go from creating a capsule wardrobe to obsessing over executing it with precision. The next thing you know I'd be out shopping for the perfect piece to round out my Pinterest-perfect capsule wardrobe.

On my very first day of minimalism, I gutted my closet. I had no plan, no system, no strategy. Just a ruthless determination to stop frittering away my one shot at life on all this stuff we thought we needed to own. I went in with a burn-it-all-down approach.

I began in one corner of my closet and worked my way across, pulling anything and everything off the hanger that I didn't absolutely love. It didn't matter if I had worn it yesterday or had never worn it at all. I didn't care if it was picked up on sale or cost way, *way* too much money. The only items allowed to remain in my closet that day were the ones I loved to wear. If it was a little too snug, too short, too itchy, or too frumpy even for me, it was gone. I was on a mission.

Giving myself fewer options just made sense now, and I was determined to become the uncluttered person I knew I was inside. I always assumed my hatred for folding laundry and hanging up clothing was the reason our closets were an overflowing, hot mess. Turns out I'm very capable; I just needed fewer things to manage.

At the end of that day, you could hardly see our bed or the bedroom floor. They were covered in piles of clothing ready to be donated. Each article of clothing was evidence of a lifetime of overconsumption and excess. I was caught somewhere between mortified and energized. I had no idea I owned that much stuff.

Once everything was finally sorted, bagged, and dropped off at its new home, I felt like a new person. It hadn't been easy, and it took more time and mental energy than I thought I could spare. But at the end of that first week, I knew a clutter-free closet was for me.

The problem, however, was that a few weeks later, it started to feel cluttered again.

PROJECT 333

While a strategy-free declutter is better than no declutter at all, I have to imagine if I had a plan in place when walking into my closet that day, I would have been able to let go of so much more from the start.

Once the dust had settled, I was left still staring at a pretty full closet. If your closet is anything like mine was, ditching over half of your clothes will *still* leave you with an overabundance of clothing. While I now loved everything I owned, I still had too much of it! My closet remained a mess, laundry still took forever, and finding what I wanted to wear was a daily struggle.

It wasn't because I had continued accumulating new items either. Not at all. I was constantly pruning my closet in small waves, letting go of more and more clothing with each pass. But it never seemed to provide the relief I was after. That's when I began to wonder if there was something to this whole capsule wardrobe thing. Maybe that Courtney Carver wasn't so crazy after all. Perhaps I was overthinking it—I mean, that's kind of my thing. What if I could approach a capsule wardrobe with the same grace I had in every other corner of my home and finally clear my closet of the clutter once and for all?

> *When creating a minimalist closet, I needed clear boundaries and strong guardrails to help me maneuver back on track when I got turned around.*

There is a difference between legalism and boundaries. Legalism is concerned with the way something appears from the outside. Boundaries, however, help protect you, sometimes even from yourself. When creating a minimalist closet, I needed clear boundaries and strong guardrails to help me maneuver back on track when I got turned around.

After two years of minimalism, I finally gave Project 333 a try, committing to wearing only thirty-three articles of clothing for three straight months. I didn't donate everything I owned less thirty-three items. I just carefully selected thirty-three items from what I already owned and committed to only wearing those things for three months.

It wasn't nearly as painful as I feared. In fact, as it turned out, I was already only wearing roughly thirty-three items anyway. The other stuff I was holding on to was hardly getting any use. You can read more about the Project 333 fashion challenge in Courtney's book *Project 333* or online at https://bemorewithless.com.

Participating in that three-month fashion challenge was a kick in the pants. It gave me the boundaries I needed and the confidence to declutter my closet for good, just as I hoped.

BUILDING A CAPSULE WARDROBE

During any given season, the number of items in my closet varies a bit. Now that I'm in the habit of having fewer articles of clothing to choose from each day, I don't pay much attention to how many articles of clothing I own. I do, however, still keep a capsule wardrobe. It's just one of the many delightful boundary lines that have helped me maintain my clutter-free closet.

The best way I've found to build a capsule wardrobe is to first decide on a base color. A base color is the foundation on which you'll select which items stay and which should go. I chose black.

Now, this doesn't mean I *only* wear black. It simply means every article of clothing I keep and purchase can be worn *with* black. The shoes I buy need to match black tops. The tops I buy should match black shoes. The pants I buy should match black tops, and so on. I do the same thing with my kids' clothes. I only buy what will match black pants. If you tend to be drawn toward blues, browns, and reds, a black base color may not be for you. Select a base color that best fits your preferred color palette.

Deciding on a base color will provide you with plenty of freedom to own what you love while simultaneously establishing the boundaries needed for halting unnecessary accumulation. Prior to creating a capsule wardrobe, I'd buy something simply because it was cute, never pausing to consider whether I had anything to wear it with. What happens when you buy cute pants that match nothing in your closet? They either sit there indefinitely or you must now purchase something to wear them with. When you use your base color as a boundary for decluttering and making purchases going forward, you'll never run into this problem.

Look for clues as to what base color would best suit you by taking inventory of what you already own. What are your current favorite articles of clothing?

Look for clues as to what base color would best suit you by taking inventory of what you already own. What are your current favorite articles of clothing? If you're already wearing your brown sandals nine months out of the year, that may be a sign that brown would make a great base color for you. If your black cardigan is getting used on an almost daily basis, black may be more your style.

Once you've chosen a base color, it's time to start building a capsule wardrobe from what you already own. Let go of the items that don't pair well with your base color, keeping your favorite items that do.

Now, in theory, a "capsule wardrobe" doesn't need to be minimal at all. You could own hundreds of articles of clothing all matching your base color if you wanted to. But if you're looking to go a little further—which I suspect you are—in order to reduce your daily decisions, enjoy a clutter-free closet, save money, and spend less time on laundry, then a *minimalist* capsule wardrobe is your best bet.

Continue to prune away the clothing you don't find yourself wearing, resist the urge to accumulate more, and practice living with less by only wearing your favorite clothes on repeat. Sometimes we worry what people will think if we don't space out our outfits. But is it really worth it? Is it worth keeping a cluttered closet to appease these imaginary people? In my experience, very few people care what you wear, and those who do aren't likely your people anyway.

Sticking to the boundaries of your base color may sound restricting at first, but it's really quite freeing once you get the hang of it. I mean, just think of how many tops go with gray ankle boots. You'll still have plenty to choose from when in need of something new. Your minimalist capsule wardrobe will simply help you narrow it down more quickly and choose what to wear with ease—even if it is a little frumpy.

HOW TO USE CHANGES IN SEASON TO DECLUTTER YOUR CLOSEST

Now that we know a capsule wardrobe isn't a painful exercise in deprivation but rather a comfortable guardrail meant to keep you on track, we're better equipped to declutter with purpose. Like I said before, decluttering your closet won't be a onetime gig. To this day, I still find items now and then that have outworn their welcome in my life. It's simply a continual process of evaluating what is essential and letting go of what is not.

> *Sometimes we worry what people will think if we don't space out our outfits. But is it really worth it? Is it worth keeping a cluttered closet to appease these imaginary people? In my experience, very few people care what you wear, and those who do aren't likely your people anyway.*

Let changes in season become trail markers reminding you to check in with what you own. A change in weather is a great opportunity to take an aerial view of what you wore and what you didn't; what you look forward to wearing and what you don't. Be sure not to misread my words here: I'm not telling you to wait to declutter your closet until the leaves start to fall or the trees begin to bud. Of course not; start today if you can. But use every change in season to take one giant leap forward. Just imagine how much clearer your closet could be one year from now if you do.

Here are three questions to keep in mind when seasonally decluttering your closet.

1. Did I Wear It?

Somehow I still manage to find one or two pieces at the end of every season that I didn't really wear. Identify the items you didn't wear this season and ask yourself, with that ruthless kind of honesty, if it can go. Sometimes there's good reason, like pregnancy or a stay-at-home order. It's not always as simple as did you or didn't you wear it. Just because you didn't wear it doesn't mean you have to ditch it; just be aware that it may.

2. Did I *Enjoy* Wearing It?

I used to wear clothes I hated all the time. As if I owed that overpriced, itchy top an opportunity to see the world. Life is too short to be needlessly uncomfortable. Go ahead and let go of the top you've been wearing out of guilt—you know, the one with the neckline you're constantly readjusting. Ditch any and all items that are just more work than they're worth. You deserve to feel comfortable and confident in the clothes you wear, even if that means you own fewer of them.

3. Is It Still in Good Condition?

Take a status report of everything you wore during this season. Do the articles of clothing still fit well? Are they in good condition? Did your daughter kiss your belly with chocolate ice-cream face and permanently stain your favorite shirt? Let go of any item that is no longer in the condition to be worn.

CURATING YOUR OWN MINIMALIST CAPSULE WARDROBE

Just the other day I discovered a hole in my jeans in, um, an *unfortunate* location. I didn't notice it until the end of the day, of course, so only the good Lord knows how long I'd been flashing the world. At times like this, letting go is a no-brainer. Other times, however, it isn't always so clear.

I couldn't possibly tell you which items should make up your capsule wardrobe. I'm currently writing this chapter while sitting on my couch, still in my pajamas, at 11:00 a.m. At this same moment in time, you might be lounging on a beach, performing heart surgery, fishing with your granddaughter, nursing an infant, teaching a classroom of graduate students, or leading a board meeting. It's tempting to want a quick-fix template to follow. But trust me: *my* capsule wardrobe won't work for you. Mimicking someone else's capsule wardrobe in an effort to shortcut your simplicity journey will likely lead you back to square one, with nothing to wear.

As of right now, my *most* favorite top is a teal, hand-me-down, button-up flannel. If you google "minimalist capsule wardrobe," you most certainly won't find a ten-year-old teal flannel in the search results. What you will find is a lot of black, white, gray, chambray, and maybe, just *maybe*, a little mustard yellow or muted mauve in the mix—but let's not get too crazy now.

A bland color pallet is just one of many misconceptions surrounding what it means to live with a capsule wardrobe. Here are few others I have heard a time or two.

- Minimalists are only allowed a certain number of items.
- Minimalists can't go shopping for new clothes.
- Minimalists must wear the same thing every day.
- Minimalists don't wear accessories.
- Minimalists only buy high-end, name-brand clothing.
- Minimalists don't wear vibrant colors.

While some minimalists do choose to wear a uniform, stay within a simple color pallet, or stick with owning just thirty-three articles of clothing, many of us don't. It's words like *only*, *can't*, *don't*, and *must* that make minimalism feel unattainable and restrictive. Know this: whatever you love to wear you can keep wearing. The goal here is not to make you *look* like a minimalist but to put your minimized closet to work for you; highlighting your individual style while simultaneously simplifying your life.

MESSY MINIMALIST TIP:
TRY A SAME OUTFIT CHALLENGE

If you're worried that wearing the same outfits on repeat will get you weird looks, dare to give it a try. Do a seven-day same outfit challenge. Tell no one, not even your significant other or bestie, and go seven days wearing the exact same outfit every day. I'm betting that nobody notices—and if someone does, it will make for an interesting topic of conversation.

17

HOW TO PASS ON MINIMALISM TO YOUR FAMILY

Kids might make minimalism more difficult in a home, but they also make it more important.

—Joshua Becker

Never, in all of my years of practicing messy minimalism, were the benefits of living with less more evident than that time we were all sheltered in place at home to help save the world. With all three kids home full time, it was the quiet I missed, not the stuff. With one exception—my hospital-issued N95 mask I had decluttered a few years prior—there was nothing we had gotten rid of that I wished I had back. I didn't need more throw pillows littering my living room. The extra summer sandals or winter sweaters I donated wouldn't have gotten used anyway because all I wore every day were leggings, a T-shirt, and slippers.

But I have to say, the award for the Least Missed Items has to go to the endless piles of toys we used to own. The last thing I needed during quarantine were more toys. My kids did a perfectly fine job of wreaking mayhem with the toys they owned.

Between the forts, the crafting, the sewing, the baking, and the generalized free-for-all, our home was pretty much always a mess. At one point, Raegan even lost a sewing needle in the art room, and we never did find it. And by "art room," I mean our dining room. We were forced to surrender that room to her craftiness once she and her art supplies earned squatter's rights.

All that to say: the pandemic didn't undermine my minimalism. In fact, it only reinforced our need for messy minimalism. Then, more than ever, we needed a home full of grace, mess, and joy. We needed the essentials and none of the excess.

A MESSY MINIMALIST APPROACH
TO RAISING MINIMALIST KIDS

During my early days of minimalism, I had high, unrealistic hopes of raising children who willingly and joyfully embraced a minimalist lifestyle. I thought that once we cleared their bedrooms of the excess, ditching 80 percent of the toys in our home, they'd look around and say, "You know what, Mom? You were right. This *is* better. Thanks!" Minimalism had made such a difference in our home and in my own demeanor that I just assumed the benefits would be as obvious to my children as they were to me.

When becoming a minimalist with kids, it's even more important to regularly check in to ensure your expectations are reasonable and your goal a realistic one. Ask yourself if what you're asking of your kids aligns with what you are hoping to gain in the long run. Remember, a picture-perfect playroom is not the goal. We're after a much larger payout here, one with fruit you may not get to harvest for years.

Becoming a minimalist family didn't look at all like I hoped. There were no thank-yous. There was no recognition of my genius. Most days they fought the idea of letting go, hard. They preferred to keep it all. They couldn't understand why too much was too much. Once again, the problem wasn't with my kids and their love of all things trinkety. No, it was with me and my ridiculous expectations.

You see, I initially held on to the belief that in order to create a minimalist home, I'd need to turn my kids into minimalists too. When they didn't happily skip along beside me to donate their unused toys after I had done the hard work of "leading by example," I felt like I was failing at minimalism.

I wanted our minimalist home to quickly and permanently mimic those idealistic picture-perfect images I saw portrayed in magazines, websites, and on social media. I wanted both my home and my kids to look the part. *Real* minimalist kids would be content playing with only a pine cone, while mine had a death grip on a mountain of plastic junk.

> *Through a lifestyle of less, our children will have a deeper understanding of who they are and what they truly treasure.*

It's important we remember as we create minimalist homes that we are not raising *minimalists*. We don't get to decide that. We're simply raising kids *in* a minimalist home. They are going to love what they are going to love. Messy minimalists aren't concerned with looking the part, fitting the mold, or making sure their kids one day call themselves minimalists too. You see, my hope now is not that when they're grown they will live in tiny houses, with minimalist capsule wardrobes and as few material possessions as possible. I don't need my children to tell stories as adults of how their courageous mother once took a stand against birthday-party favors.

No, my hope is that through a lifestyle of less, our children will have a deeper understanding of who they are and what they truly treasure. We're hoping to better equip them to choose contentment over entitlement, generosity over selfishness, faith over self-reliance, and grit over taking the easy way out. Whether they one day decide to call themselves minimalists is up to them. All I can do is light the path as I lead by example—not just with my stuff but with my soul as well. After all, I've found them to be rather intertwined.

Not a day goes by that I don't witness the countless benefits of less in my children, even if they can't yet see those benefits for themselves. While there certainly isn't a one-size-fits-all approach to creating a minimalist home, I've found grace, humility, authenticity, and patience to be absolutely essential.

The process of simplifying your home will be neither easy nor uniform. If you have multiple kids, each one of them will respond differently. The road may get rocky, unpredictable, at times even painful. Some days your entire family will walk confidently forward with you. Other days they'll moonwalk backward, and you'll be forced to carry them on your shoulders as you push on forward. Every five steps forward may be followed by two steps back. But little by little, toy by toy, moment by moment, you're going to lay a firmer foundation of contentment, generosity, and gratitude for your family.

GETTING OUR KIDS ON BOARD-ISH

Once I stopped trying to force-feed my kids minimalism, it gave way to a process that worked—not every day, but many days. In this next section, I'm going to share with you five first steps to take when becoming a minimalist family, as well as some practical strategies for helping kids let go of the excess and look first to contentment. As always, take what works for you and leave the rest behind.

1. Apologize

Every time I cleared an area of our home, I'd parade my kids in front of my donation piles in an effort to inspire them. I figured by the time we got around to decluttering their stuff, they'd be ready.

Instead, they flipped out a little. Especially my oldest. He was seven at the time and was having a really difficult time with the thought of parting with anything. He's always been the sentimental type, the kind of kid who kept the price tag from a new shirt because it had an image of a stormtrooper on it.

The more words I used to explain the benefits, the more apprehensive and suspicious he grew. He did not want to let go of a thing. We had been talking in circles for what seemed like hours when suddenly it hit me. This was all *my* doing.

For the entirety of his seven little years of life, I had modeled holding on. Who was I to now expect him to break that habit simply because I had spent three months trying to walk it back? With that epiphany I stopped trying to explain myself and instead said, "I am sorry. This is my fault..."

He listened skeptically as I took responsibility for all of it. "This is hard because for your whole life, I taught you something different. We are starting over. All of this stuff—all of this time spent cleaning and managing it all—has become a distraction." I continued, and I'm sure at some point he tapped out—I tend to ramble—but I know he heard the most important parts because it all shifted after that. He went from white-knuckling every broken toy to letting go of a few.

Hear me, friend. It wasn't always easy after that. He didn't proceed to declutter with a vengeance. That moment we laid vital groundwork that would help him take one step, then another. Sometimes forward, sometimes backward. What that apology did was shift some of the weight of letting go off his shoulders and onto mine. We carried it together. It gave him permission to lower his guard and trust that his momma wasn't out to take things from him but rather to spend more time with him.

2. Incentivize

With a little incentive, doing hard things becomes just a little easier. Decluttering with kids is no exception. While we donated most of our excess toys, we chose a handful in excellent condition to sell on

Facebook Marketplace with the purpose of raising money to put toward a fun family experience. Every time we sold an item, we'd clip the money earned in plain sight to celebrate our progress. The kids loved to watch that pile of ones grow.

After a few more months, we put that money toward an overnight trip to a waterpark. On arrival, the kids were beaming with pride knowing they were a part of making this trip happen. On our way home, I asked them what they thought. Had it been worth it? Could they recall any of the toys we had donated or sold? That moment furthered our cause in a big way because the unanimous response was, "Worth it!" None of them could recall a single item they'd let go of either. After that, I knew no matter what difficulties arose along our minimalist journey, we were doing the right thing.

> *We want our kids to see that minimalism isn't here to steal their joy. It's a tool we can use to make room for more of the things we love to do.*

Incentivizing isn't the same thing as bribing. We're not offering them new toys in exchange for old ones. It's about partnering with your kids, making them allies in your quest for less, and giving them the opportunity to see up close that experiences are far greater than accumulating excess stuff.

Brainstorm together as a family to decide on your own incentive. What would bring your family more joy than those excess toys? It can be as big or little as works for you. Perhaps it's an excursion on an upcoming trip, pizza and a new movie, ice cream, a gaming system, a trampoline, or even a pet. We want our kids to see that minimalism isn't here to steal their joy. It's a tool we can use to make room for more of the things we love to do.

3. Emphasize

As you progress, it's easy for kids to lose sight of why you started decluttering your home in the first place. It's important you bring it to the forefront of their minds on occasion.

Some days it felt as though I were commentating a live sporting event, dramatically and enthusiastically announcing things like, "Wow, it took just a few minutes to pick up the living room. That was so fast. Good thing we got rid of so much stuff. Do you want to play a game since we don't have to spend all afternoon cleaning?" In my experience, it won't take all that long for them to catch on to what you're doing and roll their eyes, but keep doing it. Partly because it's fun to annoy them sometimes, but mostly because we should seize every opportunity to reinforce the benefits of intentionally living with less.

4. Provide Clear Boundaries

Kids need to know exactly what is expected of them. Don't leave them hanging with arbitrary guidelines like "You need to get rid of some of these toys" or "I'm going to come through with a trash bag." Trust me. I've said both of those lines a number of times and it only causes them to grow anxious. It's not useful for making any real progress.

Instead, it's important to define the boundary lines for their possessions. I'd encourage you to resist the urge to give them numerical boundaries, such as "choose ten books to keep" or "give away fifteen toys," because doing so robs them of any autonomy and places the emphasis on the stuff itself. Instead, show them where their stuff goes and allow them the freedom to keep what they can store there. For example, provide a shelf or drawer for their books. When it starts to get overly crowded, have them choose a few to let go of. The same goes for toys. Each of my kids has a drawer under their bed for toys. If the toys begin to overflow, it's time to let go. This provides them with ownership over their space, freedom to accept gifts, boundaries to know when they're approaching too much, and permission to let go as needed.

You will absolutely be tempted to micromanage how they maintain that space. My son crams his bookshelf full like it's a game of real-life Tetris. While I'd much prefer he organize the books and give them a bit of breathing room, it's his space. In this case, I lean hard on the messy side of my minimalism and walk away. *Wooossah.*

5. Choose Consistency over Intensity

You're welcome to move as intensely and quickly as you'd like with your own possessions. Go ahead and fill fifteen trash bags with your own clothes and clutter in one Saturday afternoon. But if you're hoping for change that lasts with your kiddos, consistency trumps intensity every time. You must be willing to go slowly.

We can't expect children and teenagers to accomplish overnight what took us thirty-plus years to come around to. Play the long game. Being content with less will benefit them for a lifetime, but it's a lesson that can't be learned overnight. Pushing too hard or forcing them to declutter too much too fast can, in fact, have the opposite effect.

They're watching you. They're watching how you purchase, how you respond to new trends, and how you meet the needs in your community. Be consistent in your message, lead with your actions, and be willing to move at a pace that won't overwhelm them.

DECLUTTERING WITH KIDS

Once you've set aside any unrealistic expectations and taken those first five steps, it's time to assist your kids in letting go of the toys, clothing, and tchotchkes cluttering up their space. Below are seven practical, hands-on strategies for helping our kids declutter and reduce the influx of new stuff.

1. Empower Them with Choices

We know which toys our kids love and which they haven't touched in months. As you lead your kids through decluttering their toys, the words you use are critical. Present them with two toys, one they love, one you know they don't need. Then give them a choice. "How about we donate this one, but keep this one?" I've found this helps them to immediately identify their favorite items and empowers them to make a decision. Remember: they are developing their own decluttering muscles.

2. Establish a Holding Spot for Junk

When you come across random items that have run their course—such as a dentist-office prize, birthday-party favor, or bouncy ball excavated from beneath a couch cushion—place it in a hidden holding spot. We refer to the top of our refrigerator as "purgatory." There we place random toys and forgotten artwork to patiently await their fate. Once a decent amount of time has passed, and you're certain your kids have forgotten all about it, just let it go.

3. Experiment with Less

Without your kids' help, gather a small box of toys you are confident they won't miss. Then go ahead and add in a couple items they occasionally play with as well. Don't trash it; instead, hide the box, and then announce that your family is conducting a science experiment in the practice of less. Explain that you've temporarily taken some of their toys, but reassure them you will not be trashing this box without their permission. Explain that you want them to experiment with having fewer toys in their bedroom or play area. The goal is to discover if they actually have more fun in a less cluttered space, lose fewer toys, and clean up in record time.

In my experience, they'll try and fail to guess what you've taken, but don't tell them. After a good amount of time has passed—I'd suggest two to four weeks—remind them of the box, as they will have likely forgotten all about it.

When I reminded my daughter of the box, she went ahead and gave me permission to trash it. She didn't even want to see what was inside. My son, on the other hand, wanted to take a look. I figured he would. He quickly grabbed the toys I knew he would want to keep for a bit longer, and then we trashed the junk. *Wink.*

4. Maintain Traditions

Don't become a vigilante and start canceling birthday parties and eliminating Easter baskets. That's a great way to ensure your kids resent this minimalism thing. Instead, make small, subtle course changes. For example, give consumables in their Easter baskets instead of toys. Host smaller birthday parties or suggest a fun experience with just one friend. Keep the fun, just ditch the accumulation.

5. Grab a Flashlight and Get Sneaky

Remember: most kids won't embrace a minimalist lifestyle if they come home from school one day and you've trashed their stuff. That said, you can make a few larger strides now and then by grabbing a flashlight, getting sneaky, and decluttering a few random items lost beneath the bed while they sleep. (Insert maniacal laugh.)

This is just a strategy to keep moving the needle. I came across plenty of junk my kids had long forgotten about. Sometimes it's best to let them decide, knowing those small wins will help them build their own decluttering muscles. Other times, if you sense they're getting overwhelmed or bogged down by decision fatigue, it's okay to go ahead and ditch old or broken toys on their behalf. After all, this is your home. As a rule, though, never throw away something they currently play with or have loved long and hard without their permission.

6. Use Holidays to Your Advantage

As holidays and birthdays approach, take the opportunity to clear out even more, with the purpose of both "making room for new things" and donating to others in need. One fun way to motivate kids to declutter is to have them wander around the home on Christmas Eve, in search of toys they are willing to let Santa take with him to give to kids in need.

7. Set New Expectations

Your cluttered home is a result of the way you've purchased and accumulated in the past. But, my friend, today is a new day. The greatest impact you can make in your home is how you accumulate—or rather, don't—from here on out. Decluttering with a family may be slow going, but you'll make absolutely zero progress if you keep allowing the clutter in.

If you've always bought your kids three birthday presents, give just one this year. If you've always accepted every trash bag full of hand-me-downs, sift through them first and only accept the pieces you actually need. Consider creating capsule wardrobes for your kids as well. Start new habits and set new expectations for how your family approaches material possessions from now on.

BUT WHAT ABOUT GRANDMA?

It was a month or so after Christmas when we first went minimalist. Christmas 2016 was just like every other Christmas before it. *We* bought our kids so much stuff. Their *grandparents* bought them so much stuff. Their *aunts and uncles* bought them . . . So. Much. Stuff! At the end of every family Christmas gathering, we'd struggle to make all the gifts fit into our vehicle for the drive home. Once home, we'd unload it all into our living room, wrestle overly exhausted, sugar-loaded children into bed for the night, and *that's* when the real work would begin. The work of finding a home for all of our new stuff.

Now, I don't mean to sound ungrateful. I'm not. I wasn't. We know, very well, what a privilege it is to live in such close proximity to generous relatives who adore our children. But the pace at which we were accumulating stuff was simply unsustainable. Our home couldn't store it all, and my sanity couldn't take it anymore.

As you move toward implementing minimalist principles into the way you give and receive gifts, you will likely come up against some friction from family members unwilling to comply. "How do I stop the grandparents from giving my kids so many presents?" is the most common question I receive from those adopting minimalism with a family in tow. As the holidays approach, the question arises more frequently. Here are a few key strategies to lead your extended family toward gifting with greater intention.

1. Lead by Example

At the risk of sounding redundant, I'm going to talk about leading by example one last time. I promise. When people ask me how to stop grandparents from giving too many gifts, I like to do a little digging and ask a few questions in return. What I find more often than not is these frustrated, would-be minimalists have done very little to declutter their own homes. In the spirit of tough love, let me just say this: it is so not fair of you to ask Grandma to give like a minimalist if *you* have yet to do the same.

> *It is not fair of you to ask Grandma to give like a minimalist if* you *have yet to do the same.*

On top of that, it's unrealistic for us to declare ourselves minimalists the day before Black Friday and expect Grandma to get on board in a month's time. Thankfully we went minimalist in mid-January, giving us a whole year to really show our families that this was for real, that we were in this for the long haul. They witnessed our home grow clearer and watched as we, ourselves, gave our kids fewer birthday gifts with greater intention. When Christmas rolled around, they knew what to expect from us when they asked for our kids' wish lists. It is imperative we as parents go first.

2. Offer Alternatives

Don't just toss out a broad blanket request asking family members to "give fewer gifts." It will feel restricting and may have the opposite effect. Instead, offer alternative gift ideas. Suggest gifts that won't add to the clutter but instead promote connection, physical activity, adventure, and education. Get intentional and be specific.

3. Celebrate the Small Wins

When my kids come home *empty-handed* from breakfast at Cracker Barrel with Grandma, that's a big deal. I make sure to thank my parents because I know just how much my mom loves to give my kids gifts. When a grandparent gives one of your children an experience gift—a pedicure, a fishing trip, swim lessons, or archery class—instead of another toy, acknowledge it. Make sure they know just how deeply you appreciate them not adding more stuff to your home. Take it a step further and send them pictures of your children enjoying the gifted experience. It will positively reinforce what you know to be true: kids prefer experiences over things.

4. When It's Time to Put Your Foot Down

Now let's say you've been at this for over a year. You've decluttered your home. You've minimized your own holiday gifting, choosing to give experiences and consumables over the latest trending items. You've offered grandparents and extended family plenty of alternatives, grace, and more patience than you had to spare. But still the stuff train just won't stop.

What then? Well, it's time to simply put your foot down. Perhaps a firmer conversation is in order. Or maybe you go ahead and offer back the excess a few days later. If all else fails, the stuff is yours now and you can go ahead and donate what your family doesn't need.

This is your home. These are your children. You know you are doing the right thing, and your heart is in the right place. You, dear friend, do not need to live in an overly cluttered home to appease someone else. Your kids need a peaceful parent a heck of a lot more than they need an overflowing playroom. The peaceful tone in your home will be the thing they remember most when they're grown. It's the gift they are getting in exchange for not opening ten extra toys on Christmas morning.

Guard your home diligently, fiercely, and, if it comes down to it, unapologetically.

WHEN YOUR SIGNIFICANT OTHER IS NOT ON BOARD

I'm very aware of how lucky I am that my husband got on board with this minimalism thing as quickly as he did. It wasn't but a few weeks later that I found him sifting through his closet, ditching the old high school polo shirt I figured he was saving to be buried in some day.

Here's the thing. He didn't get on board because of anything I said. I didn't wow him with statistics, promise him an increase in our savings, or present a rousing speech about the benefits of raising kids in a home with fewer toys. I simply got started.

If you've got a significant other hesitant to let go of the excess, get started anyway. No, I'm not telling you to declutter their stuff without permission. Don't become a criminal. I'm saying you can still start today by effecting change in the corners of your home unique to you. Declutter your closet, your book collection, your nightstand, or your car. Let go of those thirty old nail polishes, your three backup curling irons, or your baseball card or Beanie Baby collection that, as it turns out, won't be funding your retirement after all.

Start the process on your own. Initiate your own spending freeze, find a donation site that aligns with your values, and begin letting go of the stuff you've been holding on to for far too long. While you're working to live minimally, for now, let go of the expectation that those you live with are ever going to as well. You can still become a minimalist while living in a home with those who'd prefer to call themselves maximalists; minimalism is about so much more than the stuff.

People often assume that getting their spouse on board is the holy grail of becoming a minimalist. That it becomes instantly easier after that. In my experience that just isn't the case. Sure, it absolutely helps, but to this day my husband and I often disagree on the very definition of clutter. Living as a minimalist couple is a constant practice in compromise.

He's got a couple of small drawers in the basement full of the most random things. Cords, bolts, tools, random plastic thingamajigs that go with something, but neither of us really know what. I'd love to swoop through and trash 90 percent of it, but it's just not worth it. I'm not the only one living in this house. On that same note, if he had his way, he'd come through and donate my adorable, small, well-curated collection of eclectic vintage coffee mugs. (For the record, that isn't at all how he'd describe them.) He sees those mugs as clutter while I see them as a treasure, sparking joy every morning.

Patience is your friend when it comes to persuading your spouse, kids, roommates, or anyone else you live with into minimalism. In time, as you continue to clear your life of the excess, don't be surprised if you find they're more drawn to your minimized areas within the home than their cluttered ones. Simplicity can have that effect on people.

THE UNBUSY LIFE

So where does all of this decluttering get us? We've worked to cultivate a messy minimalist mindset, reduce decision fatigue, consume more intentionally, and leave behind the idea of picture perfect. We've made great strides toward clearing our homes of clutter and living with less stuff. Our homes can now be tidied in a fraction of the time, and we're no longer stuck on the hamster wheel of organizing and reorganizing stuff.

That's all wonderful. But what's it all *for* if we don't also slow down our pace long enough to enjoy the peaceful home we've worked to create? Let's not stop at our stuff.

As we move into the final section of this book, we're going to switch gears and discuss the next important step on the path toward a simplified and meaningful life: the unbusy life. This next section is an invitation to go beyond just swapping physical clutter for clearer counters, debt for a growing savings account, or quantity for quality. Through the practice of messy minimalism, we can also swap mindless busyness and unneeded hurry for an intentionally slower pace. Our homes will never become the sanctuaries we long for if we don't give ourselves any time to actually be there.

MESSY MINIMALIST TIP: DON'T SWAP YOUR CLUTTER FOR CONFLICT

Let me say that a little louder. Don't swap your clutter for conflict! It's just not worth it. The people in your home are far more important than eliminating the excess stuff. The fewer battles you take on, the better. Minimalism won't reduce the stress in your home if you're constantly arguing about what should stay and what should go. Look for commonalities. Focus on the ways you can implement less together, and let go of the expectation that you'll ever agree 100 percent on how your minimalism plays out within your home.

PART IV

LIVING WITH PURPOSE

18

SLOW DOWN

*When you start keeping less around in your physical space,
you create space to notice more, and sometimes it results in
noticing more about yourself.*

—Melissa Coleman

It was around four o'clock in the afternoon when I pulled into my
mother-in-law's office complex parking lot with a car full of children.
Three children, to be exact. I had somewhere to be early that evening,
and Grandma, God bless her, had offered to let me drop the kids off at
her office and scoot out the door.

I ushered them in, hushing their squeals and reminding them to at least
pretend to be civilized since, after all, this was a place of employment. All
of my instructions flew out the window thanks to the large bowl of candy

sitting on her desk. I gave each of them a quick hug before making my escape. Just before sliding out the door, I assured Grandma that I'd buckle my littlest's car seat inside her truck before I left. It was the very least I could do. And that's exactly what I did. I shuffled Amelia's oversized five-point harness car seat from my vehicle into hers, just like I promised.

When we arrived back home later that evening, the kids were fast asleep. On top of that, my kitchen was spotless. I was in mommy heaven. My mother-in-law shared the details of the evening, explaining how well behaved my kids were—she'd never imply otherwise—but mentioned she encountered one little hiccup. She had to alter plans a little because I hadn't put that car seat in her truck.

I gave her the most confused look and said, "Yes I did."

To which she replied, "Um, it wasn't in there."

And just like a flashback scene in a movie, I found myself back in her office parking lot.

There were two white trucks in the parking lot that afternoon. When I left her office, I was in such a hurry—so distracted by my usual tight schedule—that I had made a costly mistake. I had yanked that car seat out of my vehicle and swung open the door of the first white truck I saw.

That's right. I had climbed inside a stranger's vehicle and buckled that car seat into it.

To this day, I can't help but laugh when I imagine the owner of that truck discovering a peanut butter–stained car seat randomly buckled into their back seat. I picture that confused driver removing it, as stale goldfish crackers pour from the cracks and crevasses onto the floor of their spotless vehicle.

One second is all it would have taken—one second for me to glance up from my hurry and notice that this was not my mother-in-law's vehicle. But I was in a rush, too focused on where I was going to bother paying attention to what was directly in front of me.

Busy has always been a way of life for me. From the moment I woke until the moment I crashed at the end of the day, I made sure I was always moving.

Now, hurry isn't always avoidable. Sometimes it's the result of your ten-year-old opting to ambush his sisters with a Nerf gun instead of brushing his teeth, putting on his shoes, and getting in the flipping car like you've asked him to do twelve times. Other times it's a necessary part of living intentionally. Purposeful projects, fender benders, flat tires, or the everyday messiness of real life makes us rush around at times. Nothing can stop that.

> *I thought I thrived when rushed, hurried, and under pressure.*
> *Because of that, I created a life that fit that narrative.*

The type of busy life I'm referring to is one that is self-induced. I used to joke that I was a stay-at-home mom who never stayed home. I made sure we had somewhere to be every single day, filling our days with outings, play dates, soccer for my three-year-old, and swim lessons for my eight-month-old. I said yes to every commitment asked of me, regardless of my bandwidth or skill set. If that wasn't enough—if I didn't *have* to be somewhere—I *found* somewhere to go. This typically landed me inside a store somewhere, shopping for more things I certainly didn't need. At the end of the day, I couldn't possibly be responsible for the state of my cluttered and chaotic home. After all, I was just *too busy* to do anything about it.

I thought I thrived when rushed, hurried, and under pressure. Because of that, I created a life that fit that narrative. I proudly embraced the busy life, believing a life of hurry was the life that fit me best. It took an intentional and forceful slam on the brakes for me to learn I don't actually thrive in a constant state of hurry after all. I don't do my best work under pressure or when under the gun. No, I was just addicted to it. Having used overly busy as a method to outrun chaos my whole life, it had become the only thing I knew to do.

Looking back, the reason I made myself so busy all of the time was to avoid addressing the internal unrest within me and around me. Busy is a distraction—and an effective one at that. If I found myself with a minute to spare, I'd feel compelled to fill it with a project, errand, or phone call. Anything that would keep me from having to be alone with myself.

Early on in my minimalist journey, I didn't truly have to slow down either. I simply replaced all of my errand running with decluttering my home. Becoming a minimalist can keep you pretty busy. At least for a while.

However, as the workload began to lift, the spaces in my home grew clearer, and I continued to intentionally hack away at my busy schedule, I was caught off guard by just how difficult it was to be alone with my own thoughts. Why couldn't I just be still? It was awkward, uncomfortable, and often accompanied by rogue waves of worry. Eventually my resistance became futile and there was nothing else to do but dive inside.

The more margin we create in our calendars, the more unavoidable our selves become. What I discovered was rough. While I had done a decent job of looking put together from the outside, I found my mind and soul in need of work. I had grown into an unteachable, worry-prone, know-it-all perfectionist who was hiding from her strengths for fear she'd actually have to use them.

Now, this isn't a book about my own personal and spiritual growth journey (well, I guess maybe it is, a little bit). I hope that any sharing on my part—about all the things cluttering up my mind and heart—will lead you to this truth: Clearing the clutter from your home and slowing down enough to savor life is a beautiful thing, but be warned. It's a slippery slope, one that will likely send you down a number of unexpected rabbit holes. Busy is often a coping mechanism, and you're going to have to investigate what it is you're hiding from.

Getting to a place where a slower-paced life fits comfortably takes time, patience, and persistence. A lifestyle that now feels like a cozy blanket on a rainy afternoon started out feeling like a straitjacket in ninety-degree heat. I hated it. Creating down time and large chunks of margin in your calendar can, at first, feel just as awkward as looking at the newly emptied corners in your home. We've grown rather accustomed to our hurried way of life.

But if you're looking for more than just a few weeks with clear counters and nowhere to be, then you're going to have to get real with yourself. You're going to have to address why, for you, the unbusy life is so uncomfortable.

I don't know exactly what you'll find as you quit the race, stop constantly moving, and plant yourself face-to-face with just you. Perhaps it's anger or fear that needs to be addressed, or a relationship you need to right, or wounds that need to be healed, or expectations you need to release. Until you're willing to turn and face the parts of you in need of uprooting, living at a slower pace will be next to impossible.

Getting to a place where a slower-paced life fits comfortably takes time, patience, and persistence. A lifestyle that now feels like a cozy blanket on a rainy afternoon started out feeling like a straitjacket in ninety-degree heat. I hated it.

For some, this may have absolutely nothing to do with something you're trying to avoid but rather a lifestyle you're working to keep up with. Perhaps you've embraced busy as a means to be the best, continuously comparing your hustle with the people around you. Our culture today is overextended. We are living hectic lives in the name of reaching greater "success." We sign our kids up for sports as soon as they can walk, hoping they'll have a better chance of making varsity. We offer up our evenings, saying yes to every new opportunity, to ensure we aren't overlooked next time. We're afraid we'll be left in the dust of other people's achievements, so we go, go, go, investing in all of the wrong things. Eventually we find ourselves sputtering along on empty tanks, with no time or energy left for the things we were actually made to do.

And that, right there, is the crux of it all. We're done. Over it. We are sick of moving through life hyperfocused on the wrong things, living into an identity that doesn't fit, and pouring our time and energy into things that don't last. We want to live lives that, in the end, matter. We want to be available to the people we love, learn more about who we were made to be, and use the margin in our calendars to invest in more meaningful activities.

Slowing down isn't about living idly. It's about living purposefully.

TRADING BUSYWORK FOR PURPOSEFUL WORK

"I'm just so grateful I've slowed my pace," I said to my husband on our way upstairs to bed after a long day at the lake. Maybe it was the sun, the s'mores, or the crackling fire, but with just over a year of minimalism under my belt at the time, I was feeling all the feels.

You'd think after over thirteen years of marriage I'd have figured out that bedtime is the *worst* time to start long, existential conversations. But for whatever reason, I never learn. I waited, expecting him to say something like, "I know, right?! You're sooo amazing, babe. I love the new you!"

He, however, took a different approach and said, "Do you *really* feel like you've slowed your pace? You've got a lot going on."

I whipped my head around, giving him a look of shock. How did he not see how super chill and cool I was these days? Had he forgotten about that crazy, overwhelmed lady who used to occupy the right side of his bed?

At first I was offended. But as I thought about it, standing on the stairs, I knew exactly what he meant, and he was right. We had gone all in during that first year of minimalism, swapping our clutter for clarity, pruning the unnecessary obligations, and enjoying the fruits of our decluttering labors. Yet as my husband had just pointed out, I hadn't decluttered my life and then maintained every ounce of margin gained. No. I had used it to start a blog, join a book club, say yes to public speaking—*gulp*—and volunteer to coach my son's soccer team. Life was far from simple, yet for some reason it felt remarkably simplified.

I lingered on the staircase, contemplating just how committed I was to proving my point; I mean, after all, I was sun soaked and exhausted. "I guess now I'm just busy about my purpose," I said, to which Paul nodded in agreement—lucky for him because I'm *always* very committed to proving my point.

There's a difference between running in circles and moving with purpose. Deciphering between the two can be tricky. Running in circles gives us the illusion of productivity. It makes us feel like we're getting something done when, in fact, we're just stuck on the hamster wheel of busywork, going nowhere.

Slowing down isn't about living idly. It's about living purposefully.

Busywork consists of things like excess laundry, reorganizing clutter, redecorating your home for the hundredth time, keeping up with changing trends, running meaningless errands, and saying yes to another volunteer task outside your skill set because you just don't know how to say no. It's signing your children up for so many activities that you can't recall the last time your family had an evening off, let alone an entire weekend.

Those are the kinds of tasks we are looking to offload through intentional simplicity and the act of slowing down. Not in an effort to remain always and forever unbusy, amen. But to create space for living meaningful lives.

A meaningful life requires we make lots of room for rest, play, and a whole lot of doing nothing because producing purposeful work requires it. You can't pour out from an empty cup. That's the sweet gift this unhurried life offers. You'll get to also make more time for the things that fill you up, which very well may include cheering your kid on from the sidelines at a sporting event. We are here to make time for the things that matter by eliminating the things that don't. We can reduce the time spent on laundry by creating a simple capsule wardrobe. We can eliminate excess errands by becoming more conscious consumers. We can streamline grocery shopping and meal planning by creating a simple meal rotation. We can stop spending our weekends reorganizing the garage, basement, or storage closet by eliminating clutter and excess once and for all. We can prune back our obligations in order to enjoy the peace that comes from a wider margin and increased bandwidth.

Now, it is possible to find yourself so comfortable in your new state of rest and slow living that you forget that the world needs what you have to offer. Don't simply trade one comfort zone for another by turning from hurrying to hermiting. Slowing down doesn't mean we prune away every hard thing to live a self-centered life of leisure.

Implementing minimalism into your calendar is ultimately about making and maintaining the margin that will offer you a greater capacity for living purposefully, undistracted, and available.

Margin → Rest → Greater Capacity → Purposeful Living

Busy → Exhausted → Distracted → Survival Mode

This is the practice of constantly pruning the dead, dying, and needless branches so that the fruit we produce will be the very best. As messy minimalists we know that trying harder, moving faster, and living hurried doesn't always lead to productive living. It's time to slow down. It's time to get specific about where we choose to spend our time and energy.

What might *you*, dear friend, do with a little more capacity in your tank? Without the burden of paying off debt from overconsumption or the exhaustion that comes from keeping pace with your neighbor? What would you pour your heart into if you stopped trying to do it all? What could more margin do for you?

Maybe it's a chance to start a business, join a ministry that's been tugging at your heart, or bake dinner for your neighbor who just had a baby. Perhaps it's an opportunity to support a cause, volunteer at your local rescue mission, become a mentor, or find a mentor for yourself. Whatever it is, it's worth slowing down for.

There's a saying that goes, "If it isn't a hell yes, then it's a hell no." It's meant to be a simple litmus test to help you decide which commitments to say yes to and which to say no to. While I do appreciate the sentiment behind it, I've found that, for many decisions in life, the yeses and nos aren't always so obvious. Sometimes the right thing to do is not an easy yes. Sometimes the right thing to do is hiding behind a fear of failure, disguising itself as a hell no.

My gut screamed "No way!" when I was asked to speak to a group of businesswomen about the benefits of minimalism. Public speaking takes a lot out of me, and businesswomen? I'm not a "businesswoman!" Yet this was something I needed to do. This was the big, scary, and brave yes that my new margin had created capacity for.

> *We are here to make time for the things that*
> *matter by eliminating the things that don't.*

When my kids' school called and asked if I'd take on the role of part-time school nurse during a global pandemic, helping to create a protocol to keep our kids and faculty safe, my first thought was, "No thank you." But again, maintaining margin now allowed me to confidently step into this role—well, as confidently as possible.

Yes, these both challenged me, stretched me, even scared the crap out of me. But remember: slowing down, learning to say no, getting uncluttered, and choosing to live with less isn't about honing our ability to avoid every hard thing. You can listen to your gut, but when your gut wants to puke, sometimes it's because she's being a scaredy cat. Don't be afraid to push back.

MESSY MINIMALIST TIP: CREATE A RESET DAY

My ability to procrastinate small tasks could earn me a medal. I can hold off on finishing even the simplest tasks from my to-do list, such as making a dentist appointment, for a shocking amount of time. It probably has something to do with my long-held belief that I work best under pressure. If this sounds at all familiar to you, try creating a reset day. A reset day (or even half day if that's all you've got) is one day a week where you get it all done. Use your reset day to put your home back in order, clean out your car, order groceries, fold the lingering laundry, and make the appointments. This allows you to procrastinate until your reset day and frees your brain from stressing about it all week long.

19

CHASING BUTTERFLIES

Wherever you are, be all there.

—Jim Elliot

A few summers back I got poison oak. On my face. Let me just tell you, it's not a good look.

You see, I've got a daughter who I'm convinced just might be part fairy. When she was little, I had to keep an extra close eye on her when we were outdoors. One moment she'd be running through the sprinkler, and the next she'd be three houses down, chasing a butterfly. That's just the kind of girl she's always been: a whimsical noticer.

To this day, chasing beautiful bugs is still one of her favorite pastimes. She's been known to spend entire weekends rescuing dragonflies from spiderwebs, hoping to nurse their web-bound wings back to full health. I hate to admit that although I am a nurse, the Crawford Dragonfly Hospital has an embarrassingly high mortality rate.

Her whimsy can be rather contagious, so one particular afternoon when she asked me to join her outside to chase butterflies, I couldn't say no. At the time I was in the middle of folding laundry while listening to a podcast. I stopped what I was doing, turned off the podcast, slid my phone into my back pocket, and headed outdoors.

Raegan sprinted out ahead of me and began darting across our yard, from corner to corner, chasing these small, elusive butterflies. She didn't have a net, a jar, or a plan; whimsical fairy children rarely do. Based on what I could see, we weren't actually going to be *catching* any butterflies today; only chasing them.

I followed her back and forth for a few minutes before my eye caught a cluster of weeds on our property's edge. As she ran to and fro, I started pulling weeds. "I mean, if I'm going to be out here," I thought, "I may as well make the best use of my time." Of course, Raegan tried to protest as I turned our adventure into a chore—to which I replied, "Nooo, I'm totally still playing! I'm just going to get rid of these weeds while I wait for a butterfly."

Eventually I remembered how much I hate pulling weeds and paused to check my phone instead. I replied to a few texts, made a quick phone call, and eventually started to feel a little guilty. Was I truly unable to engage in the seemingly simple task of chasing butterflies with my daughter? I slid my phone back into my pocket and set off in hot pursuit.

But it was too late. The damage had already been done. No, I'm not referring to a permanent fracture in our mother-daughter relationship. That's the thing about whimsical fairy children: they're very forgiving. But thanks to my inability to just chase the butterflies, coupled with my lack of botany knowledge and obvious phone addiction, I ended up with poison oak on my hands and face. That's what you get for making phone calls while weeding.

It took a good couple weeks for that rash to completely disappear, but the lesson—along with a heightened fear of all things landscape-related—has stuck with me. This is what happens when I try to do two things at once. I end up doing them both badly, and I often find myself worse off than when I began. I used to think I was quite good at multitasking. I mean, very little evidence backed this theory, and if you ever watched me attempt to hold a conversation while making a grilled cheese sandwich, then you know just how false that claim was. I do, however, have a pretty good handle on how to scrape the burned parts off a charred grilled cheese so a toddler will eat it (#lifeskills).

> *We've got to stop sacrificing the moments that matter on the altar of busyness because we just don't know when to quit, when to rest, when to play, and when to say no.*

That's not good enough, though. We shouldn't settle for a life spent losing our car seats, liberally applying hydrocortisone cream, and scraping away the parts we let burn. We've got to stop sacrificing the moments that matter on the altar of busyness because we just don't know when to quit, when to rest, when to play, and when to say no.

Your life deserves your full attention. In order to give our days the attention they deserve, we've got to learn how to decipher which things are worth our time, which things are not, and then learn to say yes and no with confidence.

When someone asks you to do something, what is the first thing you say? I'm going to go out on a limb and guess that it probably sounds something like this: "Hmm, let me look at my calendar, and I'll get back with you." Does that sound about right? But it isn't our literal, physical availability on a particular evening we should first consider; it's our capacity, our bandwidth. Bandwidth is the energy or mental capacity required to deal with a situation. Are you hanging on by a thread? Feeling pulled in one million different directions? Do you have anything left to give right now? It's vital that we assess our capacity as much as we do our calendars.

It doesn't matter if that day is wide open in your calendar; if your bandwidth is rapidly fading, the answer should be no. Plenty of things can contribute to the depletion of our bandwidth: busy seasons, family drama, illness, financial stress, parenting, getting ready for back to school, or even just getting your kids out the door in the morning *for* school. It all pulls from our internal bandwidth.

In order to maintain a full tank, we've got to stop making commitments based on our physical availability and remember to first check in with our capacity. Filling every sliver of your schedule will run you ragged fast and even put you at risk for resenting the commitments you were actually once excited about.

There have been many times when I've said yes to something, even when I knew I couldn't take on one more thing, because I just didn't have the tools to say no. If we're going to show up wholeheartedly and fully present—if we're going to avoid pulling poison oak when we should be chasing butterflies—we've got to find the words to say no.

When confronted with a potential commitment, instead of just saying yes or no, I had gotten into the habit of saying maybe. I'd say something like "let me check my calendar" or "let me talk with Paul, and I'll get back with you" in an effort to buy myself more time to figure out how to Houdini my way out of an ask. Saying no from the start seemed too harsh.

Deep down, I think I was hoping for an easy out. Perhaps there would be a national crisis, a zombie attack, or, more likely, a puking child to give me "permission" to say no. In the meantime, the decision would weigh on me and add unnecessary stress to my already overwhelming mental load. Paying close attention to the state of your bandwidth and knowing you need to decline is one thing; actually doing so is another story. After thirty-plus years of "let me check my schedule," the words flow from my lips before I even have time to think. So instead of kicking myself over it, I've added one little line to the end of my response—one that changes the script altogether. It gives my words a whole new meaning. I now say, "Let me check my schedule . . . and see if I have the capacity to take that on right now."

Eh? See what I did there? This way, my answer isn't about how full my calendar is but rather how full my tank is. I've made it an issue of my *sanity*, not my availability—and that, friend, is hard to argue with. While our calendars and physical availability are certainly important variables to evaluate, looking only at your schedule will land you deeply lost in the land of busy.

Know this, my messy minimalist comrade: you won't get it right every time. Even to this day, I find myself in over my head from time to time, wondering how I got myself into this mess. Yet the more you practice saying no, the more quickly you'll begin to recognize when you need to, and the more confident you'll grow with doing so.

BOUNDARIES

A few years back my husband and I did that "word of the year" thing to help ring in the new year. In case you've never heard of it, this is an exercise meant to help you clarify your goals for the year. Choosing a word means thoughtfully deciding on a theme for your coming year. I've heard people choose words like *determination*, *consistency*, and *rest* to help prioritize their one specific goal for the year, whatever that may be.

We included our two older children in this activity as well, which was very entertaining. Of course they tried to choose words like *football* and *candy*. But as we talked it through, they eventually landed on more meaningful words. One chose *focus* and the other chose *brave*—though I do think they likely spent more time and energy focused on watching football and bravely eating candy that year, but we'll take what we can get.

I chose the word *balance*, and I spent that year working to obtain it. At the time I was getting my blog off the ground, and I was hoping to find the perfect way to balance this new work with my family life. But the harder I tried to find this thing called balance, the more spun-out I felt.

When I was working, I felt as though I should be with my kids. When I was with my kids? Well, you know how it goes: can't live with them, can't live without them.

During the course of that year, searching for perfect balance, I learned a lesson far more valuable than the one I was after. Balance isn't a thing. I mean, I guess it's technically a thing. If you've ever suffered a bout of vertigo or tried to hold the standing tree pose during a yoga class, then you know balance is an *actual* thing. But when it comes to prioritizing your life, you'll always find perfect balance just out of reach.

What I really needed that year were better boundaries. Did you know the word *priorities* is a relatively new word? According to Greg McKeown in *Essentialism*, "The word *priority* came into the English language in the 1400s. It was singular. It meant the very first or prior thing. It stayed singular for the next five hundred years. Only in the 1900s did we pluralize the term and start talking about *priorities*. Illogically, we reasoned that by changing the word we could bend reality. Somehow we would now be able to have multiple 'first' things."

Instead of trying to balance the chaos, cramming as much into my day as possible, I've started drawing delightful boundary lines around one priority at a time. Some people might refer to this as "time blocking," which is a time-management method designed to make you super productive. But those words make my face start to twitch. I immediately go into fight-or-flight mode at the very thought of time blocking my day because my every previous attempt at doing this has failed miserably. Why, you ask? I got too specific. I went hour by hour and made a rigid, inflexible, picture-perfect schedule to block out my entire day. I never managed to stick with it, and I always ended the day feeling like I'd failed. It's surprisingly difficult to muster up an ounce of creativity when you've allotted a sixty-minute window to do just that. It's like trying to fall asleep at night when you just can't turn off your mind. You start counting down the minutes until the next hour thinking, "Okay. If I fall asleep now, I'll get six hours of sleep. Okay, if I fall asleep now, I'll get *five* hours of sleep." Impossible.

Instead, we should theme large portions of each day based on our most pressing priority—around what is most important this day. For example, if it's work related, I'll carve out half of the day to dedicate only to that. I don't reply to messages, take phone calls, or arbitrate arguments between my children. If Mom is on a deadline, it's *Lord of the Flies* around here.

Other times an entire day or even a whole weekend needs to be devoted to spending time with my husband and our children. This is especially true when I feel my bandwidth blinking Low Power.

Choosing a *theme* for an entire day or even half of the day is especially helpful for people like me who have a difficult time compartmentalizing but have perfected the art of overthinking. To theme your day is to narrow your focus, minimize distractions, and lower your overall expectation while maximizing productivity. Stop trying to juggle it all and instead choose one thing to hold on to at a time. One single priority.

It's important to remember that a well-themed day must be held loosely. If we get knocked down every time life changes our plans, we'll never accomplish anything. Don't freak out; get flexible. I was in the middle of writing this book when the pandemic shut down the world. I had been making great progress, functioning well with a routine that allowed me plenty of uninterrupted writing time. I was convinced this uninterrupted writing time could only take place in the morning and that my brain turned to mush in the afternoon.

Well, after being thrust into the role of remote learning facilitator overnight, my lovely little plan went out the window. At first, I panicked. It's kind of what I do. Panic first, think later. After a mild tantrum, I realized I had two options. Fail epically at fulfilling my first-ever book deal, or become an afternoon writer. I chose the latter.

Hold it all loosely and be willing to pivot when necessary.

DIGITAL MINIMALISM

The area of my life most in need of firm boundaries is how often I check my phone—which, according to research, is between five times an hour and every twelve minutes. If I don't decide ahead of time exactly how I'm going to use my time, nine times out of ten I'll dwindle it away scrolling through social media.

If my phone is within arm's reach, odds are good I'm going to check it. *Often.* Probably more frequently than every twelve minutes some days. I know I'm not alone either. I messaged ten friends just this morning to ask them this: "What do you see as the biggest source of distraction in your everyday life?" (Let's not overlook the irony that I stopped working to text ten friends, with my phone, so I could write about how problematic phone addiction can be.) Every last one of those friends I texted, without fail, said their phones are their biggest source of distraction. If we aren't careful, if we aren't intentional, we'll let our phones keep us from our real lives. Heck, your phone might even leave you with poison oak on your face.

> *Rather than assuming you need a new closet organization system, or a better calendar, or a more detailed outline for your day complete with thirty-minute bullets for time blocking, ask yourself this: What needs to go?*

When I feel that phone buzz in my back pocket, I can't not check it. Perhaps there are better people out there than me—those who, like Frodo from *The Lord of the Rings*, can resist the urge. But I'm more like Sméagol. (*My precious.*) I've even toyed with the idea of getting a flip phone and ridding myself of this too-smart-for-its-own-good phone once and for all. But how would I ever fall asleep to watching reruns of *The Office* for the hundredth time?

All this to say, I don't have this digital minimalism thing completely figured out. Clearly. I do, however, know this: the problem isn't just our phones; they are merely the latest shiny object dangling in front of us.

Every moment offers us a new opportunity to fully engage, yet we continue to let our phones pull us from our present moments into virtual ones. It's important we get clear on our priority: our first, most important priority in that moment.

We've got to decide ahead of time how we are going to spend our time and establish the boundaries to do just that. Whether it's deleting apps, turning off notifications, dedicating specific hours to respond to messages, or placing your phone on top of the refrigerator when you get home from work until after the kids go to bed: boundaries give us the freedom to bring the best of us into what is essential in each moment.

It's eighty degrees out right now. I'd love to shut this laptop and head out fishing with my kids, but right now, in this moment, I know I'm exactly where I'm supposed to be. I've dedicated these hours to this chapter. It is my priority, so here I sit. Thanks for the company.

MAKE A HABIT OUT OF LESS

If you find yourself overworked, overcrowded, overhurried, and overburdened, look to *less*. (Well, look to Jesus, then look to less. But in my experience, Jesus is much easier to locate when fewer distractions are clouding up my vantage point.)

I want you to picture your calendar the same way you picture your physical space. Organizing an overly busy schedule is just as difficult as trying to organize an overly cluttered kitchen. Eventually you run out of places to cram things, and you're forced to start shuffling the overflow around in plain sight. Just as the problem in your kitchen has very little to do with your space, your cluttered calendar has little, if anything, to do with the concept of time itself. The problem isn't the number of days within a week or hours within a day; the problem is how much you're trying to make fit.

When you find yourself asking questions such as "Why is this area of my home always a disaster?" or "Why are we always running in a million different directions, with no time left to relax together as a family?" ask yourself a different question. Rather than assuming you need a new closet organization system or a better calendar or a more detailed outline for your day complete with thirty-minute bullets for time blocking, ask yourself this: What needs to go?

We've gotten in the habit of doubling down when we face too much. It's time to try a new approach. Instead of doubling down, getting up earlier, and hustling harder, find something you can eliminate. Start training your brain to work smarter, not harder. Every time you find yourself overwhelmed, stressed out, or too exhausted to do the things that matter, look around for something you can let go of. Whether that be a dried-out marker, evening commitment, unrealistic expectation, or weekly playdate that has begun to feel more like a burden than a blessing, it's time to replace the habit of more with a habit of less.

MESSY MINIMALIST TIP:
IT'S OKAY TO FINISH WHAT YOU START

"The dishes can wait," they say, "but life won't." Well you know what? Sometimes the kids can wait. That day my daughter asked me to chase the butterflies, I needed to fold the laundry, but instead, I walked away with poison oak on my face.

When we're in task mode, accomplishing something that needs to be handled, it's difficult to pivot out of that and be fully present. It's perfectly acceptable to just say, "I can't right now." That's how we keep to-do lists from lingering and our minds from getting cluttered with unfinished tasks. Finish what you started, then get out there and chase the butterflies.

You know by now that a little mess never bothers me. Here's the thing, though. Parenting today isn't like it was when we were younger. Moms in the '80s and '90s weren't inundated with social media images and parenting articles reminding them of the fleeting hourglass of motherhood. Sure, I want to chase all the butterflies I can while my babies still live within my home. That's a large part of why I've simplified every possible facet of my life. But until someone invents an affordable version of Rosie from *The Jetsons*, I'm still going to have to fold some laundry from time to time.

20

A MESSAGE FROM
THIS SIDE OF CLUTTER

You can't go back and make a new start, but you can start right now and make a brand new ending.

—James R. Sherman

I've spent the last couple weeks writing and rewriting the final chapter of this book. I must have written it a dozen times over. This chapter has taken hours of my life, given me more than a couple headaches, and caused me to stand in front of my pantry, stress-eating grain-free granola right out of the bag. (That's right, I said grain-free granola! It's all we had, which should provide for you a true testament of my desperation. Moving on.)

You see, I wrote the beginning of this chapter months ago. It began with a really great story, one I was very committed to keeping in this book. I thought it fit perfectly here. Yet no matter how I wrote it, rearranged it, or rephrased it, it just didn't fit. The longer I worked to try to fit it in, the more committed I became to keeping it. I even tried changing the entire point of the story, but nothing worked. I thought the story was important, if only I could find a place for it to go.

Eventually I reached the end of my rope, completely overwhelmed and out of both words and snacks. That's when I remembered a piece of writing advice from the famous novelist Stephen King, which I read in his book *On Writing*. He says this: "Kill your darlings, kill your darlings, even when it breaks your egocentric little scribbler's heart, kill your darlings."

> *Minimalism means putting down what you don't need so you can pick up what you do. Every layer you eliminate will reveal something new, something you've lost along the way, something money can't buy.*

Don't worry, it's not as tragic as it sounds. Stay with me. King is saying this: when writing, never remain so committed to a beloved character, story, or even one really great line that you're unwilling to cut it if it needs to be cut. It's important to recognize when it's time to walk away, let go, kill off a character you've grown to love, or delete a great story. So that, in the end, you can write a better one.

That's exactly what we're doing when choosing messy minimalism. We're taking on a posture of possibility. We're letting go of the clutter to open up our arms, our spaces, and our lives so that a more meaningful ending can start to unfold.

Ultimately, this is about making an exchange. A beautiful one. As you move through your home, don't focus your gaze on the things you're giving up but rather on what you're gaining in return. Minimalism means putting down what you don't need so you can pick up what you do. Every layer you eliminate will reveal something new, something you've lost along the way, something money can't buy. In the end, you won't be standing there empty-handed. Far from it. This exchange always tends to give more than it takes. And I'm not just referring to a missing game piece at the bottom of your junk drawer or your husband's wedding ring hiding in a jar of coins.

Your most valuable finds will look more like

generosity, buried beneath "just in case";
purpose, lost behind monotony;
curiosity, beneath a need to know it all;
presence, behind distraction;
peace, beneath chaos;
gratitude, hiding beneath never enough;
grace, behind perfection;
authenticity, behind a facade;
joy, underneath control;
adventure, behind fear;
resourcefulness, underneath overpreparedness;
creativity, lost behind fitting in;
faith, under self-reliance;
contentment, beneath entitlement;
community, behind busyness;
rest, beneath keeping up with the Joneses; and
an abundant life, beneath an abundance of stuff.

Every time you make the decision to sit with difficult emotions rather than using shopping as a distraction, every time you choose to give something away to someone who needs it now rather than hold on to it for someday, every time you choose contentment over keeping up or embrace the mess instead of fixating on looking the part: every time you do these things, you're making an exchange. It's you choosing a clutter-free life over a distracted one. It's you intentionally deleting a portion of the story to make room to write a better ending.

STAY ALERT

I'm not a big fan of air travel. Which is a nice way of saying that I absolutely hate getting on an airplane. Don't get me wrong. I've never let my fear of flying keep me from going anywhere. I suck it up and get on that plane because this world is too big and beautiful to stay put over a few hours of heart palpitations. But I don't have to like it.

My dread could be due in part to the fact that I'm a Type Six on the Enneagram (otherwise known as the Loyalist, who loves security and assurances of safety and steadiness). Or maybe it's because I just don't have a deep understanding of the science behind how an airplane manages to remain in the air. Then again, it may have more to do with the fact that as a child I watched the 1990 made-for-TV movie *Miracle Landing*. In this movie—which, I'll have you know, is based on a true story—you watch as a hole quite literally begins to rip open in the top of the airplane. The next thing you know the entire ceiling of the plane is missing, and everyone on board is holding on for dear life. I can still picture it. (I mean, come on, where were my parents?)

I've heard speculation that eventually airplanes are going to be flying themselves, with no pilots. No thank you. I can't imagine that kind of technology would be very good for business either. I don't care if that pilot spends the entirety of the flight working through a sudoku book while a computer pilots the plane. (For the record, I'm very aware that isn't at all what a pilot does.) Customers, like myself, need to know there is a human in that cockpit capable of taking control during unexpected times of rough air—or, you know, in case part of the ceiling begins to spontaneously peel away.

We've grown rather infatuated with this automated mindset. Yet what works well for robotic vacuums and slow-cooking pulled pork doesn't really cut it when lives are on the line. We can't automate a meaningful life. We've got to remain awake, alert, intentional, purposeful.

It is far too easy to spend our lives living on autopilot. We'll graduate from high school, maybe even college, get a job, and then jump in line behind everyone else. We start to run after the things this world tells us hold value, crafting our lives to look like everyone else's. I want you to stop for a moment, quiet your soul, lift your head, and look around (both literally and figuratively) and ask yourself: Is this where I want to be? Is this what I want to be living for?

Now, if you're currently reading this at the back of the school pickup line in ninety-two-degree heat, or in the waiting room at your dentist's office, then I'm sure you could picture a number of places you'd rather physically be right now. I'm not talking about logistics, nor am I suggesting you abandon your family to go all *Eat, Pray, Love.* This is about stepping into your life, not running away from it.

> *The world doesn't need one more person to mirror their neighbor or to showcase perfect. It needs you, all of you.*

You can't do anything about yesterday or the decisions you made to get you to today. You can, however, choose to alter your course. You can choose to let go of the distracted life so that in the end you will have not only written a *better* story but the story you were created to write.

This is it, friend: this is your one life, and you deserve to live it clutter-free. It's not going to be perfect, and it's absolutely going to get messy. But when you decide to get intentional, you can make it 100 percent yours.

Remember: the world doesn't need one more person to mirror their neighbor or to showcase perfect. It needs you, all of you. The uncluttered, authentic, purposeful version of you. It needs your messy moments far more than it needs the picture-perfect ones because that's how we connect. It's in our weakness, not in our greatness, that we are strong. Let's wake up to the smoke and mirrors that is our culture's mantra of more. The stuff, after all, isn't what makes a life well lived.

A CLEARER PATH BACK TO YOU

The benefits of messy minimalism reach much further than coat closets, craft cupboards, and basement storage rooms. If you let it, messy minimalism will change you from the outside in.

Ultimately, what I hope messy minimalism will offer is a clearer path back to you. Beneath it all, I want you to find not just your long-lost favorite T-shirt but who it is you were created to be. Not the version you were *told* to be but the version you were *made* to be.

> *You are a clutter-free person. Perhaps you've gotten a little off track and taken a bit of a detour. That's okay; I did the same thing. If I can work my way back, trust me, so can you.*

Let's stop wasting time by chasing what will always remain out of reach, whether that be staying ahead of changing trends or keeping a perfectly curated minimalist home. Picture-perfect minimalism may look nice from the outside, but man, it's the maintenance that'll get ya. The upkeep will suck the possibility right out of the sweet gift of less. While you may no longer be hyperfocused on material possession, perfection will distract you just the same. In the end, the messy minimalist way of life might *look* a whole lot like minimalism, except here we purposefully sidestep the trapdoors of perfectionism and comparison that minimalists have a tendency to fall through.

Last, I've got a little secret to share.

You, dear reader, have what it takes to live this messy minimalist life. In fact, you've had it in you all along. Just like Dorothy, you've been rocking those ruby-red slippers the whole time. I wrote this book not to give you the strength to get uncluttered or to even show you how; I wrote it to remind you of who you are and to point out the trail markers along the path you're already on. You are a clutter-free person. Perhaps you've gotten a little off track and taken a bit of a detour. That's okay; I did the same thing. If I can work my way back, trust me, so can you.

Unfortunately, getting uncluttered does require a bit more effort than a simple click of the heels. It is, however, very much worth the work and time spent. In the end, as time passes, your space is cleared, your calendar boasts a bit more margin, and the benefits compound, that hard work part will grow a little fuzzy. In time, the moments of frustration and the weekends spent sifting will become a blur, and it may just feel as though all it took was a click of the heels after all.

Welcome to the world of messy minimalism. It's a place where we get to ditch both our extra cookie cutters as well as the idea of ever becoming one. Here there's no such thing as perfect—just grace. An abundance of it.

ACKNOWLEDGMENTS

For some reason, I found this tender section of the book to be the most difficult to write. The perfect words to express the fullness of my gratitude for those who helped bring this book to life simply don't exist. Writing and publishing this book was a *whole* thing, only further complicated by a global pandemic. I could have never done it without the relentless support of so many.

Endless thanks to my husband, Paul, for supporting me, and this book, in more ways than I can count. Thank you for loving me, knowing me, rooting for me, giving me the space to freak out on occasion, and showing me how to be a little more Enneagram Three than Six when necessary.

To my three favorite children on the planet, Jameson, Raegan, and Amelia. This project wouldn't have been possible without you and the messes you leave behind. Thank you for cheering me on and fending for yourselves from time to time. Your overwhelming enthusiasm during the highs and your patience during the thick of it helped bring this book to life.

To my editor, Valerie Weaver-Zercher. I can't thank you enough for giving me the opportunity to make this dream a reality. This book is better off because of you and your remarkable attention to detail.

Thank you to my family and dearest friends for supporting me, encouraging me, and celebrating every win, even while I shut myself away, ignoring your texts for months on end.

Thank you, thank you, thank you to . . .

ACKNOWLEDGMENTS

My very first "editor," Stacey Salow, for saving me from myself when it comes to everything from grammar to fashion.

Becky Lowe, for continuously reminding me I have what it takes to finish this book well.

Effie Alofoje-Carr, for calling it early and never letting me doubt.

My watercooler friends, Denaye Barahona, Erica Layne, and Zoë Kim. Thank you for your support, encouragement, inspiration, and occasional kick in the pants.

The readers of *Abundant Life with Less*. It's a beautiful thing to find your people. I can't thank you all enough for your support over the years and for making this a community that feels like home.

Finally, but most importantly, I want to thank God for showing me a better way and always reminding me that He's not finished with me yet.

NOTES

CHAPTER 3

28   **"In the words of author Jon Acuff":** Jon Acuff, "Be Brave Enough to Be Bad at Something New," *Jon Acuff* (blog), August 3, 2020, https://acuff.me/16081/.

CHAPTER 4

32   **"The ultimate form of intrinsic motivation":** James Clear, *Atomic Habits: An Easy & Proven Way to Build Good Habits & Break Bad Ones* (New York: Avery, 2018), 33–34.

34   **"Writes Erica Layne":** Erica Layne, *The Minimalist Way: Minimalism Strategies to Declutter Your Life and Make Room for Joy* (Emeryville, CA: Althea Press, 2019), 150.

35   **"Subject of identity and the clutter-free life":** Greg McKeown, *Essentialism: The Disciplined Pursuit of Less* (New York: Crown Business, 2014), 226–27.

CHAPTER 5

39   **"The results of a study":** Darby E. Saxbe and Rena Repetti, "No Place like Home: Home Tours Correlate with Daily Patterns of Mood and Cortisol," *Personality and Social Psychology Bulletin* 36, no. 1 (January 2010): https://doi.org/10.1177/0146167209352864.

40   ***"Physicist Albert-László Barabási"***: Albert-László Barabási, *Bursts: The Hidden Patterns behind Everything We Do, from Your Email to Bloody Crusades* (2010; repr., New York: Dutton, 2011), 125.

CHAPTER 7

61   ***"She says this"***: Marie Goff, *Love Lives Here: Finding What You Need in a World Telling You What You Want* (Nashville: B&H Publishing Group, 2017), 52.

63   ***"In The Story of Stuff"***: Annie Leonard, *The Story of Stuff: How Our Obsession with Stuff Is Trashing the Planet, Our Communities, and Our Health—and a Vision for Change* (New York: Free Press, 2010), 161.

63   ***"Leonard says this"***: Leonard, 162–63.

CHAPTER 8

71   ***"Only 3.7 percent"***: Mary MacVean, "For Many People, Gathering Possessions Is Just the Stuff of Life," *Los Angeles Times*, March 21, 2014, https://tinyurl.com/yvxddcx9.

71   ***"More than doubled in size"***: Margot Adler, "Behind the Ever-Expanding American Dream House," NPR, July 4, 2006, https://tinyurl.com/fhc7hzsw.

71   ***"The self-storage industry"***: Leonard, *The Story of Stuff*, 147.

71   ***"Municipal solid waste generated"***: "Textiles: Material-Specific Data," Facts and Figures about Materials, Waste, and Recycling, United States Environmental Protection Agency, accessed April 2, 2021, https://tinyurl.com/8u4fs5mh.

71   ***"Americans each throw away"***: "Why Recycle Shoes and Clothing?," About Us: Global Responsibility, World Wear Project, accessed March 26, 2021, https://tinyurl.com/4k3v7pae.

77   ***"In his book How to Be Rich"***: Andy Stanley, *How to Be Rich* (Grand Rapids, MI: Zondervan, 2013), audiobook, chapter 3.

78   ***"Up to five thousand today"***: Caitlin Johnson, "Cutting Through Advertising Clutter," CBS News Sunday Morning, September 17, 2006, https://tinyurl.com/yr7pjss4.

CHAPTER 9

81 **"In this study":** Sheena S. Iyengar and Mark R. Lepper, "When Choice Is Demotivating: Can One Desire Too Much of a Good Thing?," *Journal of Personality and Social Psychology* 79, no. 6 (2000): 996–97, https://doi.org/10.1037/0022-3514.79.6.995.

82 **"When the options are few":** Sheena Iyengar, *The Art of Choosing* (New York: Twelve, 2011), audiobook, chapter 6.

82 **"Participation rates dropped":** Sheena Iyengar, "The Choices before Us," May 4, 2020, in *Hidden Brain*, hosted by Shankar Vedantam, podcast, MP3 audio, 10:32, https://tinyurl.com/5rv7jbbv.

82 **"Thirty-five thousand decisions":** Dr. Joel Hoomans, "35,000 Decisions: The Great Choices of Strategic Leaders," *The Leading Edge*, Roberts Wesleyan College, March 20, 2015, https://tinyurl.com/6a7vk72e.

83 **"Baumeister's research shows":** John Tierney, "Do You Suffer from Decision Fatigue?," *New York Times Magazine*, August 17, 2011, https://tinyurl.com/s3aazuw2.

84 **"He told reporter Michael Lewis":** "Barack Obama to Michael Lewis on Presidential Loss of Freedom: 'You Don't Get Used to It—at Least, I Don't,'" *Vanity Fair*, September 5, 2012, https://tinyurl.com/nw6xtks4.

CHAPTER 11

98 **"Jon Acuff says it well":** Jon Acuff, *Finish: Give Yourself the Gift of Done* (2017; repr., New York: Portfolio, 2018), 20.

CHAPTER 12

110 **"An article by Joshua Becker":** Joshua Becker, "How to Become Minimalist with Children," *Becoming Minimalist*, May 10, 2010, https://tinyurl.com/6ucenn49.

114 **"Haven't read even part of a book":** Andrew Perrin, "Who Doesn't Read Books in America?," Fact Tank, Pew Research Center, September 26, 2019, https://tinyurl.com/3ajx9kty.

CHAPTER 14

125   ***"This is how he describes it":*** Joshua Becker, *The Minimalist Home: A Room-by-Room Guide to a Decluttered, Refocused Life* (Colorado Springs: WaterBrook, 2018), 47, 116.

CHAPTER 19

186   ***"According to Greg McKeown":*** McKeown, *Essentialism*, 16.

187   ***"According to research":*** Asurion, "Americans Don't Want to Unplug from Phones While on Vacation, despite Latest Digital Detox Trend," press release, May 17, 2018, https://tinyurl.com/3vvk4z87.

CHAPTER 20

192   ***"Kill your darlings":*** Stephen King, *On Writing: A Memoir of the Craft,* 20th anniversary ed. (New York: Scribner, 2020), 222.

195   ***"That we are strong":*** 2 Cor 12:10.